SThe Year inOAPS

The Year in SOAPS

Rod Townley

CROWN PUBLISHERS, INC.
New York

Published by Crown Publishers, Inc., One Park Avenue, New York, New
York 10016 and simultaneously in Canada by General Publishing Company
Limited

Manufactured in the United States of America

Library of Congress Cataloging in Publication Data

Townley, Rod.
   The year in soaps.

   1. Soap operas—United States—Plots, themes, etc.
I. Title.
PNI992.8.S4T68   1984   791.45'75'0973   83-23229
ISBN 0-517-55323-6

10 9 8 7 6 5 4 3 2 1

First Edition

Contents

PN
1992.8
.54
T68
1984

Credits and Acknowledgments

An especially warm thanks to Ellen Howard and *Soap Opera Digest*; to Lee Sharon Fryd of NBC; to Janet Storm of CBS; to Alice Serrano and Madeline diNonno of ABC; and to John and Sandy Gabriel. Thanks are due as well to Diane Blackman of Nichols Associates, Meredith Brown of *Soap Opera Digest*, CBS's Ed Devlin, the valuable research contained in Robert LaGuardia's book, *Soap World*, Luna Carne-Ross, Beth Milstein, Gary Morgenstein, Agnes Nixon, Petronia Paley, Allen M. Potter, Jon-Michael Reed, ABC's Jenny Davis, Anne Marie Riccitelli, Elvera Roussel, Jill Yager, NBC's Hal Bender, Owen Comora, Joe Richutti, Pat Schultz, Natalie Tiranno, CBS's Gail Plautz, Jim Sirmans, and Mary Stuart.

All photographs are courtesy of the three networks and may not be reproduced without the express written permission of the appropriate network and the following individual photographers:

Cathy Blaivas: *pages 77 (top), 79.*

Bob D'Amico: *pages 37, 38, 42 (top), 46 (bottom), 47, 48, 49 (top), 50 (top), 51, 52.*

Steve Fenn: *pages 5 (top right, top left, bottom), 14, 15, 16 (top), 17, 19, 20, 23, (top left), 24, 28, 29, 31 (bottom), 32 (top), 33, 34, 35, 36 (top), 62 (bottom), 63 (top), 66 (bottom), 67, 68 (bottom), 69 (top left), 75, 76 (right), 81 (bottom), 82, 83, 85 (bottom), 86 (top), 87 (bottom), 88, 101, 102 (bottom), 104 (bottom), 105 (top), 106 (top).*

Ann Limongello: *pages 5 (middle), 6, 11, 16 (bottom), 22, 23 (top right), 69 (bottom), 72 (bottom), 74, 76 (left), 102 (top), 103.*

Joe McNally: *pages 59, 64 (top), 72 (top), 89 (top right), 90, 93 (top), 94 (top), 95 (top), 97.*

Gary Miller: *pages 89 (top left), 89 (bottom left), 95 (bottom), 69 (top right), 73 (top), 78, 81 (top), 84, 85 (top), 87 (top).*

Kevin Mulvey: *pages 89 (bottom left), 94 (bottom), 100 (top), 105 (bottom).*

Lynn Pelham: *page 73 (bottom).*

Steve Ross: *page 93 (bottom).*

Bob Sacha: *pages 8, 9, 10, 22, 23 (middle), 23 (bottom), 26, 69 (middle).*

Donna Svennivick: *pages 13, 18 (top), 27, 31 (top), 32 (bottom), 50 (bottom), 53, 54, 56, 57, 58, 60, 62 (top), 64 (bottom), 65, 66 (top), 68 (top), 77 (bottom), 92, 98, 104 (top).*

Dorothy Tanous: *page 96.*

Brigette Wiltzer: *pages 41, 42 (bottom), 44.*

THE YEAR IN SOAPS is a production of James Charlton Associates.

Designed by Mary Kornblum.

Introduction

Heat in the 90s could not deter some ten thousand soap opera fans from turning out for the largest soap festival of all time, held in Washington, D.C. last July 30. Over seventy soap stars showed up for the all-day event sponsored by the USO and Soap Opera Festivals. An 8 A.M. meet-the-stars breakfast at the Sheraton-Washington was followed by visits by the stars to various army bases and VA hospitals in the D.C. area. The van I hopped into held, among others, *All My Children*'s Julia Barr, *Another World*'s Petronia Paley (alas, the only black star in attendance), Eileen Davidson (the long blonde taffy-pull from *The Young and the Restless* who looked sultrier than the weather itself), and her boyfriend, Nicholas Walker of *Capitol*. So much conspicuous good looks in so confined a space, it was unnerving. And all kept in good spirits despite perspiration, the press of waiting fans at Fort Belvoir, even a traffic ticket!

In the afternoon there was a visit to the White House, where Press Secretary James Brady greeted the stars. This was followed by a pep rally in the great Ellipse, where the heat beat down to beat the band. "Grueling," commented *Ryan's Hope*'s John Gabriel afterwards.

With evening, events turned chic: a formal dinner in support of the USO followed by a gala reception during which soap opera memorabilia were donated to the Smithsonian Institution. Among the relics soon to find a place beside Archie Bunker's chair and Judy Garland's ruby slippers: Joanne Tourneur's little blue apron (circa 1951), an early symbol of good-wifeliness on *Search for Tomorrow*; Bert Bauer's original housecoat and coffee pot from *Guiding Light*; the hourglass from *Days of Our Lives*; and from *General Hospital*, an invitation to Luke and Laura's wedding.

Soap opera has thus officially made it into the pantheon of American popular culture. Anyone present at that afternoon's rally out in the Ellipse would have marvelled at the intensity of emotion that possesses many soap fans. Tears and screams accompanied some of the shouted questions:

Q. Erica, are you ever going to get revenge on Lars Bogard?

A. Well, my cosmetics company is going to wipe him right off the map!

Q. I'd like to ask Denise Alexander, how come they never let you wear pants on the show [*General Hospital*]?

A. It's not them. If you could see my rear end you wouldn't *want* me to wear pants on the show. I'm a basically tall person from here up, and then I have these three inch legs.

Q. I'd like to ask Alfred [*AMC,* played by Bill Timoney] if he's ever going to take off his glasses and quit being such a squirrel?

A. Alfred is coming back from Europe in the fall and he's going to be a changed man. *[Screams from audience.]*

Q. For David Mason Daniels [*Capitol*], what's happened to Carolyn Jones? We all miss her.

A. We all miss Carolyn, too. Carolyn had to leave the show because of illness. So we're all praying for a speedy recovery.

Only a few days after the soap festival, the elegant Miss Jones died of cancer. In February 1983, another actor, *Another World's* Bob Christian, also died of cancer. These were two somber events in an extremely eventful year. Two-time Emmy winner Dorothy Lyman (*AMC's* Opal) left for prime time and NBC. The loss was to an extent redressed by the temporary reappearance of Sandy Gabriel as *AMC's* scheming Edna Thornton.

There were batches of weddings, probably the most unusual being Tom and Margot's come-as-you-are affair on *As the World Turns,* though a close second must be Nola's hitch-hike on a firetruck to her wedding with Quint on *Guiding Light.* There was even an unexpected live show, for the first time in many years, when the tape for the August episode of *Search for Tomorrow* was discovered missing. It happened that newcomer Cain DeVore (playing Danny Walton) was making his debut on the show that day. (You don't suppose that *he* . . . ?)

For fans of the all-popular *General Hospital,* the big news in the fall of '83 was the six-week return engagement of Genie Francis as Laura. "I love Laura as much as my fans love Laura," she said at an ABC press conference in October, "and I wanted to end it in a proper way. . . . Laura's had a tragic life, and I want to see her . . . go off very happy." If her reported six-figure compensation can bring happiness, Ms. Francis must also have gone off with joy in her heart.

Tony Geary can feel satisfaction as well. He decided to leave the show after five sensational years as Luke Spencer. Although he expressed appreciation for the "cocooned and nurtured environment" which the show provided him, he'd been growing somewhat restive in the part and felt that it was time to move on.

Nineteen-eighty-three was a year of special ferment in the yeasty world of daytime television. ABC launched (June 27) a brand-new soap called *Loving,* scheduling it in an unprecedentedly early time period, while NBC readied a new soap of its own, *Scruples,* for possible launch in '84. NBC hit a low point after dropping *The Doctors,* maintaining only three soaps on the air, compared with CBS's four and ABC's six. Not surprisingly, ABC led the field in ratings points and in Emmy Awards. The network won 15 daytime Emmys to NBC's 10 and CBS's 8. Robert Woods (Bo Buchanon on *One Life*) won outstanding actor; Dorothy Lyman (*AMC*'s Opal Gardner) won outstanding actress; Darnell Williams (Jesse Hubbard on *AMC*) won best supporting actor; and Louise Shaffer (Rae Woodard on *RH*) best supporting actress. *One Life* took the best direction award and, as is becoming a habit, *Ryan's Hope* was honored for outstanding writing.

A final twist during this unusual year was the reappearance of a cancelled soap opera, NBC's ill-fated *Texas,* which in October was cut into half-hours for cable showings over Ted Turner's superstation in Atlanta, WTBS. Potentially these re-showings could reach millions of fans, those that missed the show the first time around, and those who want to relive the episodes they watched two years ago.

The goal of *The Year in Soaps* is to help fans relive the experiences of 1983. Cast lists, plot lines and profiles of the major characters are here, with an arrivals and departures section that covers important newcomers and leave-takers. In all, it was a memorable year for soap opera, that most maligned of art forms which yet inspires the fiercest loyalty in its fans. And now the Smithsonian! Does that mean respectability? Ph.D. dissertations? Phooey, who needs it? Just get another pot of coffee going, *All My Children* is about to come on.

Key to Abbreviations

AMC	*All My Children*
ATWT	*As the World Turns*
AW	*Another World*
DOOL	*Days of Our Lives*
Edge	*The Edge of Night*
GH	*General Hospital*
GL	*Guiding Light*
One Life	*One Life to Live*
RH	*Ryan's Hope*
Search	*Search for Tomorrow*
Y&R	*The Young and the Restless*

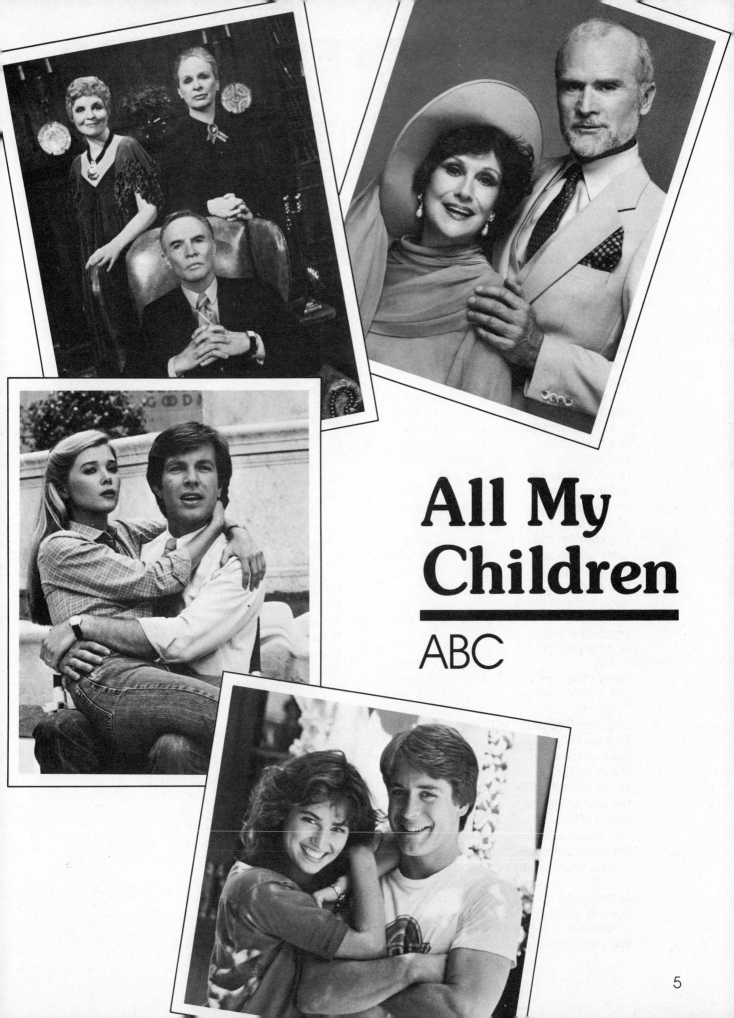

All My Children

ABC

5

The Cast

Julia Barr .... *Brooke Cudahy*
Amanda Bearse .... *Amanda*
Peter Bergman .... *Dr. Cliff Warner*
Jack Betts (briefly in the
    fall) .... *Lars Bogard*
Vasili Bogazianos (left
    in December)......... *Benny Sago*
Kay Campbell .... *Kate Martin*
David Canary .... *Adam Chandler*
Lee Chamberlain ...... *Pat Baxter*
Susanna Dalton .... *Dr. Sally Perkins*
Kim Delaney .... *Jenny Gardner*
Ronald Drake........... *Jasper Sloan*
Candice Earley .... *Donna Cortlandt*
Louis Edmonds .... *Langley Wallingford*
Antonio Fargas .... *Les Baxter*
Mary Fickett .... *Ruth Martin*
Hugh Franklin (left in
    late fall) .... *Dr. Charles Tyler*
Sandy Gabriel
    (reappeared in
    fall) .... *Edna Thornton*
Robert Gentry .... *Ross Chandler*
Lee Godart (left in
    spring)................ *Kent Bogard*
Deborah Goodrich (left *Silver Kane*
    in spring)............. *(Connie Wilkes)*
Frances Heflin .... *Mona Tyler*
Eileen Herlie .... *Myrtle Fargate*
Jason Kincaid .... *Sam Brady*
Michael Knight .... *Tad Gardner*
Mark LaMura............ *Mark Dalton*
Laurence Lau .... *Greg Nelson*
Elizabeth Lawrence ..... *Myra Murdoch*
Viveca Lindfors (left in
    fall) .... *Simone*
Susan Lucci .... *Erica Kane*
Dorothy Lyman (left in
    late fall) .... *Opal Gardner*
Ray MacDonnell .... *Dr. Joe Martin*

Milly Mack .... *Carl Blair, Jr.*
Matthew
    McNamara........... *Bobby*
Steve McNaughton
    (started
    midyear) .... *Gil*
Taylor Miller............. *Nina Warner*
Robert Milli (left in
    fall) .... *Lars Bogard*
James Mitchell .... *Palmer Cortlandt*
Debbi Morgan.......... *Angie Hubbard*
Peg Murray (started in
    fall) .... *Olga*
Kathleen Noone........ *Ellen Dalton*
Donna Pescow (came
    and left in fall)....... *Lynn Carson*
Tricia Pursley (returned
    in spring)............. *Devon McFadden*
Dack Rambo (left in
    fall) .... *Steve Jacobi*
Natalie Ross .... *Enid Nelson*
Michael Scalera........ *Joey Martin*
Richard Shoberg .... *Tom Cudahy*
Thomas Sminkey .... *Harold Loomis*
Gillian Spencer......... *Daisy Cortlandt*
Nicholas Surovy .... *Michael Roy*
Lynne Thigpen (started
    in fall) .... *Aunt Flora Baxter*
Bill Timoney.............. *Alfred Vanderpoole*
Tasia Valenza (started in
    fall) .... *Dottie Thornton*
Richard Van Vleet....... *Dr. Chuck Tyler*
Marcy Walker........... *Liza Colby*
Ruth Warrick .... *Phoebe
                      Wallingford*
Lisa Wilkinson .... *Nancy Grant*
Darnell Williams........ *Jesse Hubbard*

Producer: *Jacqueline Babbin*
Directors: *Jack Coffey, Henry Kaplan,
           Sherrell Hoffman*
Writers: *Agnes Nixon (creator) and
         Wisner Washam manage a
         stable of dialogue-writers.*

Background

All My Children, one of TV's most popular and issue-oriented soaps, was the 1970 brainchild of Agnes Nixon, creator of *One Life, Search,* and *Loving*, cocreator of *ATWT*, and one-time head writer for *Guiding Light* and *Another World*. Many fans feel that *AMC*, with its strongly defined characters such as Erica Kane, Phoebe (Tyler) Wallingford and Opal Gardner, remains Mrs. Nixon's finest creation. She herself ascribes much of the force of those characters to excellent acting. James Mitchell, for instance, says Mrs. Nixon, brings more individuality to the role of Palmer Cortlandt than anyone could "write into" the part. Be it as it may, Pine Valley U.S.A., with its Tylers, Martins, Cortlandts, and others has become one of the best-loved towns on television.

The Story

Nina Warner's in a tight spot—she's in Hawaii on a business trip accompanied by Steve Jacobi, to whom she's wildly attracted, and her husband Cliff, to whom she feels loyal. Well-intended Cliff suggests setting up Steve with Brooke. The plan makes Nina very jealous, especially when Steve finds Brooke attractive.

The chemistry between Nina and Steve becomes irresistible and they make love passionately. Unfortunately, Cliff is outside the door and hears moans within. When Nina gets home, Cliff blows up at her and vows to leave her. He wants a quick Caribbean divorce. Nina, crushed, tries to win him back.

Meanwhile, the rivalry between Erica and her sister Silver continues. Erica is trying to trap Kent into marriage; Silver slinks up to him and seduces him. Silver also fouls up Erica's appointment calendar and gives her wrong messages. She doesn't want that new "Erica" line of cosmetics to come out. She also warns Kent that Erica's trying to get pregnant by him.

Underaged Jenny Gardner is thrilled when Greg proposes to her, but her mom, Opal, thinks a richer man would be better. Jenny postpones the wedding a few months, until she turns eighteen.

Angie's and Jesse's growing love runs into even more vehement opposition, from Angie's dad, Les. Les drags Angie home and confines her to quarters when he learns she's gone to hear Jesse sing at the Steampit. Ultimately, Les realizes he's lost control of his daughter and his wife, Pat, and he moves out.

Then there are Donna's marital problems with Palmer, who has been to New York on a fling with Daisy (she plans to become the next Mrs. Palmer Cortlandt; Donna, however, won't divorce him).

Phoebe Wallingford confronts Palmer about his lack of concern for little Palmer John, Donna's child. She tells him that she knows the truth: the baby isn't Palmer's (he's sterile), it is Chuck's! Soon after, Nina learns that her mother, Daisy, is Palmer's mistress. Can't Palmer keep *any* secrets?

Poor Opal can't either, it seems. The man she cares about, Sam, finds out about her affair with con-man Langley Wallingford and leaves her. Then Opal discovers that Langley's wife Phoebe is *not* at death's door after all, so Opal won't become Mrs. Wallingford and get Phoebe's money. For revenge, she locks Langley in the sauna and incinerates his clothes. Langley is left limp but alive.

Silver continues sabotaging Erica's career—trying to make Erica doubt her own sanity—until Kent's father Lars demands that Erica be fired from Sensuelle. Lars is no sweetheart himself; he's been Ellen's lover and tries to trick her into divorcing Mark. His schemes backfire and have the effect of bringing Ellen and Mark back together.

When Opal finds out she's not going to be the next Mrs. Wallingford, she's fit to be tied.

Silver turns from mouse to louse as she tries to sabotage Erica's career. What dirty trick will she try next?

Nexus is the setting for social intrigue when this glamorous group shows up. Erica and Silver flank Kent, while Ellen is squired by Lars.

A tragic accident will soon destroy Jenny and Greg's dream of marriage.

Young troublemaker Tad Gardner returns to Pine Valley, bilks the Martins, torments Alfred and tries to bed every girl in sight. Indirectly because of him, Greg takes a bad fall and is temporarily paralyzed. Greg's mother Enid nastily manipulates the gravely ill Greg into breaking off his engagement with Jenny. It will be a long time before their misunderstandings are resolved, and meanwhile, Opal's old beau, Sam, falls in love with Jen.

The plot quickens as Cliff divorces Nina; Langley's true identity (Lenny Wlasuk, a crook) is revealed to several people but not to Phoebe; Jesse and Angie secretly marry; Brooke and Tom are reconciled. Then in a wonderfully terrible turn of events Erica gets into a jealous rage over Silver and Kent and accidentally shoots Kent. When he dies, Silver tells the police Erica killed him in cold blood. Afraid of facing the chair, Erica escapes and hides in a boarding house, where she is ultimately arrested.

Phoebe learns that Palmer connived to have Donna's baby aborted, and that he might have succeeded were it not for Chuck, who is the real father. Phoebe convinces Donna of the truth of all this and offers her the use of her home. There Phoebe protects Donna and the baby from the outraged Palmer.

Tad, meanwhile, discovers that Silver's an imposter—her real name: Connie Wilkes—and he blackmails her for $10,000. Eventually, Silver/Connie is taped admitting that the shooting of Kent was an accident. She's arrested and Erica is cleared. Fired from Sensuelle, Erica starts her own cosmetics company (with Palmer's backing) and commissions a writer, Michael Roy, to ghost her autobiography. She also gets possession of a brooch which belonged to Kent—it contains the secret of Lars's past.

Lars, meanwhile, is locked in competition with Palmer over the favors of Daisy. Through Erica, the men seem to be rivals in business as well. Mark and Ellen have their own problems, because Mark has become addicted to cocaine. Brooke faces a more immediate danger. A deranged fan named Harold Loomis tries to get close to the young TV correspondent and eventually abducts her. Frightened but compassionate, Brooke convinces Loomis to let her go.

Not everything works out so well for others. Angie becomes pregnant but still hasn't told her parents about her marriage to Jesse. When her dad, Les, finds out he throws such a fit that Angie decides maybe she should divorce Jesse to keep peace at home.

Then the worst kind of tragedy strikes when a robbery at The Chateau leads to a consuming fire which kills little Palmer John, Phoebe's beloved great-grandson. Chuck blames himself for the disaster, but Donna's reaction is worse: she doesn't admit that the child is dead. She carries a rag doll around saying 'I won't let them bury you.' Only Phoebe is strong enough to force Donna to face the truth. She takes her to the cemetery to see the grave. Donna breaks down and sobs in Phoebe's arms.

The course of true love has never run smoothly for Angie and Jesse. Can their marriage survive her father's opposition?

The Steve/Nina/Cliff triangle continues to reverberate, although Cliff finds solace in the arms of Devon while Nina and Steve fly off together in a small private plane for an intimate vacation. Later, on the return trip, the plane crashes; Steve is badly hurt but thrown clear. Approaching medics spot a woman still inside the wreckage but before they can reach her the plane explodes.

At the hospital a grieving Cliff works to save Steve's life. Glancing up from the operating theater Cliff is stunned to see Nina! The woman on the plane was not Nina after all.

Jenny and Greg have still not found their way back together, and their chances are further endangered by Jen's skyrocketing modeling career, especially when publicity hype pairs her with pretty boy Tony Barclay as "America's dream couple." Tony soon falls hard for Jenny and before long (still for publicity purposes) they say they're engaged. Greg, meanwhile, is still recovering from his injuries and is just learning to walk again. Amanda tries unsuccessfully to win his love.

Palmer is out to ruin his rival, Lars Bogard, who has just become engaged to Daisy. Lars is equally intent on getting hold of the brooch which Erica has in her possession. Ultimately, a shocked Palmer and Erica discover the photo of a Nazi officer (somewhat resembling Lars) inside the brooch. They also suspect that Olga is in league with Lars. Later, in fact, it is revealed that she is his sister. A quick trip to Argentina convinces Palmer and Erica that Lars is indeed the Nazi officer in the photo, but he's had plastic surgery so that no one will know he's a mass murderer.

Benny's step-daughter, Dottie Thornton, has shown up in Pine Valley and very soon puts the make on Jesse, much to the dismay of the pregnant Angie. Jesse doesn't particularly appreciate Dottie's advances (reportedly to the relief of a large number of soap fans who wrote in protesting the interracial storyline). Dottie's trashy mother, Edna, shows up in Pine Valley and quickly begins stirring up trouble of her own.

Another storyline that viewers reportedly had trouble swallowing was the growing friendship between gay therapist Lynn and heart-broken Devon. The poor girl has irretrievably lost Cliff once Nina refuses to marry Steve. It is when Devon asks to stay with Lynn for a while that Lynn tells her about her sexual orientation.

In the late fall, Lars confesses his Nazi past to his fiancee, Daisy, then attempts to strangle her. In the struggle, she manages to push him over the terrace balcony and he lands with a sickening thud far below. Lars's hired assassin is at that same moment stalking Palmer and Erica aboard Palmer's huge yacht, which is the scene of a high-fashion engagement party for Jenny and Tony. Jesse overpowers the assassin; then Lars himself shows up on the boat—not dead after all!—and he tumbles overboard and drowns after a struggle with Palmer.

Jesse hears that Angie is giving birth and he rushes to the hospital

These happy days will be a thing of the past once Daisy learns of Lars's Nazi connections.

moments after Angie has given their son up for adoption. He vows to find the baby. He'd also like to slug Angie's father, Les, for causing all the trouble between him and Angie in the first place. Jesse then throws Dottie out, furious that she kept her knowledge of Angie's pregnancy from him until it was too late. Jesse and Angie are reconciled and ultimately find their baby son and *steal* him back.

Greg, meanwhile, finally tells Jenny the truth about their breakup: He had only pretended to blame her for his accident because he didn't want her to pity him. Just as Greg and Jenny are beginning to rediscover each other, Jenny's fiance-of-convenience, Tony, walks in and refuses to leave. Furious with him, Jenny breaks off their engagement. Tony runs to Olga, who is furious at the possibility that all that wonderful publicity about the engagement might have been for naught. She orders him to intercept a love letter Jenny has written to Greg. Through mischance Greg doesn't get the letter, and a sad Jen agrees to marry Tony. At last the letter turns up, and Greg rushes to New York to stop the wedding which is already in progress. Arriving at the last instant, he and Jen are reunited!

Erica is delighted to learn that Adam Chandler, president of Unirest, wants to make her autobiography into a movie. Naturally, Erica can think of no one better than herself to play the lead role, and she tries her usual wily tricks to land the part. But to no avail. Near the end of 1983, Erica meets the mysterious Adam Chandler, who is financing the movie. Will he be her new romance?

The heartbreak continues. Devon, who in her young life has been through a tortured affair, a loveless marriage, a bout with alcoholism, and an unwanted pregnancy, decides that she loves her gay counselor, Lynn. But Lynn with great tact tells Devon it isn't so. She only thinks she loves Lynn, because of all the disappointments she's had with men. Liza's in an even worse situation than Devon: she's just found out about Tad's affair with her mother. She breaks off with Tad, and seems well along the road to a nervous breakdown.

Profiles

Julia Barr
(Brooke Cudahy)

Her role in *Girl in My Soup* with Van Johnson got her an Actor's Equity card; her portrayal of Charles Adams's daughter in *The Adams Chronicles* helped make her name in television. Then Indiana-born Julia Barr broke into soaps, playing the conniving Reenie Szabo on *Ryan's Hope* for five months before joining *All My Children* as Brooke. In 1981, she left daytime TV for a year to tour with Katharine Hepburn in *West Side Waltz*, but has now returned to *AMC*. In private life, she cooks, takes singing lessons, and plays the wife of Dr. Richard Hirschlag, an oral surgeon.

Peter Bergman
(Dr. Cliff Warner)

A "Navy brat," Peter Bergman was born in Guantanamo Bay, Cuba, where his dad was stationed. He got hooked on acting playing Hook in an eleventh grade production of *Peter Pan*. He stuck with the dream, studying acting in New York and eventually landing parts in *Guiding Light* and *Love of Life* before joining *AMC* in 1979.

Kim Delaney
(Jenny Gardner)

Born in a suburb of Philadelphia, Kim set out for New York City and a modeling career after graduating high school. Looks, luck, and spirit landed her in commercials and soon led to her part in *All My Children*, in 1981. She's made her off-Broadway debut in *Loving Reno*, directed by Dorothy Lyman, who plays Kim's mom on *AMC*.

Candice Earley
(Donna Tyler Cortlandt)

The road from Texas to Broadway led Candy Earley through drama courses at Trinity University, in San Antonio, to the San Francisco Company production of *Hair*, and finally to the Broadway production of the same play. She made her TV debut in *AMC* in 1976 and for a while played at the same time in the Broadway production of *Grease*. A professional singer and dancer, Candy has also performed in off-Broadway productions.

Laurence Lau
(Greg Nelson)

Young Larry grew up in a small Oregon town and majored in theatre at Utah's Brigham Young University. Persistence led to guest appearances in *The Waltons*, *Happy Days*, and other TV shows before he landed the part of Greg on *AMC* in 1981. Larry is a skier and a serious student of karate.

Susan Lucci
(Erica Kane)

The most famous vixen on daytime TV is played by a happily married mother of two. Her daughter, Liza Victoria, was born in 1975, and her son Andreas Martin, in 1980. Susan Lucci has been on *AMC* from its inception in 1970, but has also appeared in the film *Young Doctors in Love*, and in several prime-time TV shows. For three years running, she was nominated for an Emmy as outstanding actress in a daytime drama.

Taylor Miller
(Nina Cortlandt Warner)

A native of New Orleans, Taylor studied drama at Tulane and later worked as a model in Texas. In Dallas she played her first professional role, that of Sorrel Bliss in Noel Coward's *Hay Fever.* She arrived in New York in March 1979, and within two months landed her role on *AMC.* On days off, she still does some modeling, and enjoys horseback riding in Central Park.

James Mitchell
(Palmer Cortlandt)

Before undertaking the commanding (and demanding) role of Palmer on *AMC* in 1979, James Mitchell played leading parts in several Broadway musicals, including *Carnival* and *Paint Your Wagon.* He has appeared in films (notably *The Turning Point,* in which he played the artistic director), and from 1969 to 1973 he played Professor Hathaway on the daytime series, *Where the Heart Is.*

Debbi Morgan
(Angie Hubbard)

While attending high school in New York's South Bronx, Debbi got involved in workshops run by the Negro Ensemble Company and the New Federal Theatre. Soon she found herself on Broadway in Ron Milner's *What the Wine Sellers Buy*, and then toured with the show's national company. Not long after that, she was persuaded to move to California, where she met a casting director for Norman Lear's Tandem Productions. This break led to several TV appearances, but her greatest stroke of fortune came when she was chosen from hundreds of other actresses for the part of Elizabeth Harvey in *Roots: The Next Generations*. Debbi is married to actor Charles Weldon and again lives on the East Coast, where *All My Children* is taped. She joined the show in 1982.

Kathleen Noone
(Ellen Dalton)

As a youngster in upstate New York, Kathleen Noone was a talented trombone player, and later a promising night-club singer. After collecting an BFA degree-from West Virginia University she decided to throw her energies into acting, and enrolled as a graduate student in theater at Southern Methodist University. She played in several soaps (*Love of Life*, *ATWT*, *One Life*) before joining *AMC* in 1978 as Ellen.

Richard Shoberg
(Tom Cudahy)

Before joining *AMC* in 1977, Michigan-born Dick Shoberg played Mitch Farmer on *Somerset* and Kevin Jamison on *Edge of Night.* He also appeared in the TV movie, *The Silence,* with Richard Thomas. A singer and writer of songs, Dick Shoberg performs occasionally in New York clubs with Richard Hirschlag and Hirschlag's wife, Julia Barr, who plays Tom Cudahy's wife Brooke on *AMC.*

Ruth Warrick
(Phoebe English Tyler Wallingford)

Miss Warrick has come a long way from St. Joseph, MO. Her most remarkable early achievement was playing Orson Welles's wife in the movie classic, *Citizen Kane* (no relation to Erica). This led to a score of other films, a long run on TV's *Peyton Place,* five years on *ATWT,* and other TV appearances before joining *AMC* in 1970 as the inimitable Phoebe. Her autobiography, *The Confessions of Phoebe Tyler,* written with Don Preston, was published in 1980.

Darnell Williams
(Jesse Hubbard)

Winner of the 1983 Emmy award for best supporting actor in daytime drama, Darnell Williams has come a long way in a short time. Born in England, educated in the States, he landed roles in a Los Angeles production of *Selma* and in *Guys and Dolls* in Las Vegas. In New York he appeared off-off-Broadway, then made the jump to TV: *Rich Man, Poor Man, Sammy & Company, White Shadow,* and *Tom Wolfe's L.A.* He also appeared in an "ABC Afterschool Special" called *The Celebrity and the Arcade Kid,* based on Twain's *The Prince and the Pauper.* He joined the cast of *AMC* early in 1981.

Arrivals and Departures

Hugh Franklin
(Dr. Charles Tyler)

In 1950, the story goes, actor Hugh Franklin decided to retire and run a general story in Connecticut. But he soon began to miss the smell of the greasepaint and headed back to New York City, where he appeared on Broadway with the likes of Helen Hayes, Constance Bennett, Ethel Barrymore, Eva LeGallienne, the Lunts, and Sir John Gielgud. He also appeared in several movies, including *The Swimmer,* and a number of daytime dramas (*Dark Shadows, Secret Storm, Love of Life, Young Dr. Malone*) before becoming an original cast member of *All My Children.* By late 1983, the dignified white-haired actor decided that he wasn't getting much storyline and left the show. It is possible that he might make an occasional return appearance in the future.

Sandy Gabriel
(Edna Thornton)

Married to John Gabriel, *Ryan's Hope*'s Dr. Seneca Beaulac, Sandy made her own soap splash several years ago when she embodied the conniving Edna Thornton on *AMC*. She left the show to spend time raising her two daughters, Melissa and Andrea, and is now rejoining *AMC* on a trial basis.

Dorothy Lyman
(Opal Gardner)

How do you keep them down on daytime TV after they've won two Emmies? Ms. Lyman was snapped up by NBC, where she is already starring on *Mama's Family,* and was reportedly given a honey of a contract, including time off to pursue her other theatrical endeavors. A native of Minneapolis, Ms. Lyman directed Off-Broadway's *A Coupla White Chicks Sitting Around Talking.* She hasn't had much time to sit around, herself, having appeared in five daytime soaps in the course of her rising career.

Robert Milli
(Lars Bogard)

The villainous Lars could not be left at large indefinitely, and it was no surprise when he was killed off in the fall. By that time Robert Milli had already left, displeased (it is said) to learn that the character he was playing was really a Nazi war criminal. Another actor, Jack Betts, had to finish out the role for him. Now in his fifties, Robert Milli has had a long and successful stage career. On Broadway he played Horatio to Richard Burton's Hamlet, and he starred as Endicott in the 1969 revival of *The Front Page*. He has appeared in some eighteen Shakespearean productions (playing Hamlet twice) and has been seen on *Guiding Light*, *One Life*, and *Another World*.

Dack Rambo
(Steve Jacobi)

Good looks don't hurt. A farm boy from California, Dack and his late twin brother Dirk had just graduated from high school when they went to L.A. to visit an aunt. Loretta Young spotted the boys and in short order signed them to the cast of *The New Loretta Young Show*, on prime-time TV. Dack then seriously studied acting at Lee Strasberg's Actor's Studio and elsewhere, and went on to become a regular in the serial, *Never Too Young*. He later costarred with Walter Brennan in ABC's *The Gun of Will Sonnett*. He's done several feature films and TV movies, and has turned into a real soap idol as sexy Steve Jacobi on *AMC* since joining the cast early in 1982.

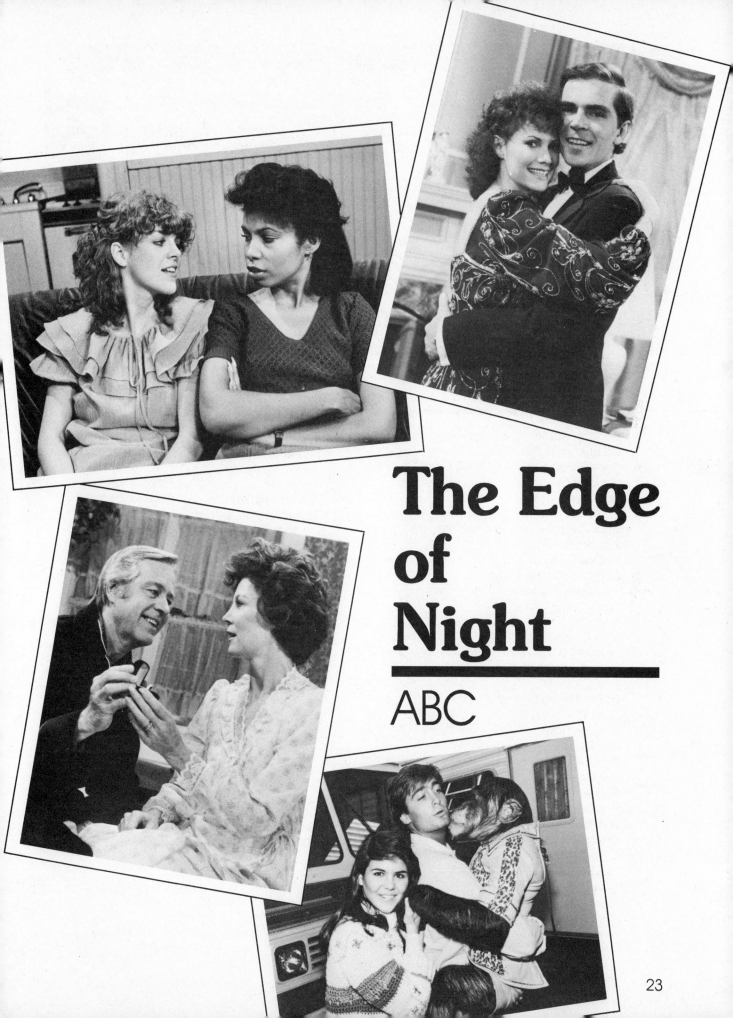

The Edge of Night

ABC

The Cast

Mariann Aalda......... *Didi Bannister*

Willie Aames (new this
year, left in fall) ..... *Robbie Hamlin*

Mark Arnold............ *Gavin Wylie*

Leah Ayres (left
show) .... *Valerie Bryson*

Susan Bigelow .... *Barbara*

Richard Borg (left
show) .... *Spencer Varney*

Catherine Bruno (left
show) .... *Nora Fulton*

Ronn Carroll (new this
year) .... *Stan Hathaway*

Alan Coates (left
show) .... *Ian Devereaux*

Forrest Compton....... *Mike Karr*

Joel Crothers........... *Dr. Miles Cavanaugh*

Sandy Faison (new this
year) .... *Dr. Beth Corell*

Charles Flohe .... *"Preacher" Emerson*

Ann Flood .... *Nancy Karr*

David Froman.......... *Gunther Wagner*

Sharon Gabet.......... *Raven Whitney*

Robert Gerringer (new
this year) .... *Del Emerson*

Lela Ivey............... *Mitzi Martin*

Christopher Jarrett (left
show) .... *Damien Tyler*

Lois Kibbee............. *Geraldine Saxon*

Caroline Lagerfelt ..... *Patricia*

Mary Layne (left
show) .... *Camilla Devereaux*

Irving Lee.............. *Calvin Stoner*

Lori Loughlin (left in
fall).................. *Jody Travis*

Larkin Malloy.......... *Sky Whitney*

Karen Needle (left
show) .... *Poppy Johnson*

Peter Nevins (on and
off show this
year) .... *David Snell*

Dennis Parker .... *Derek Mallory*

Norman Parker (left
show) .... *David Cameron*

Pamela Shoemaker
(new this year) ...... *Shelley Franklyn*

Lisa Sloan (left
show) .... *Nicole Cavanaugh*

Michael Stark .... *Sully*

Jennifer Taylor (new
this year) .... *Chris Egan*

Ernie Townsend .... *Cliff Nelson*

John Vickery .... *Richard Scanlon*

Chris Weatherhead
(new this year) ...... *Alicia Van Dine*

Jerry Zaks (new this
year, left in fall) ..... *Louis Van Dine*

**Executive
Producer:** *Erwin Nicholson*

**Associate
Producer:** *Jacqueline Haber*

**Assistant
Producer:** *Catherine Maher*

Directors: *John Sedwick, Richard
Pepperman*

**Head
Writer:** *Lee Sheldon (replacing Henry
Slesar)*

**Associate
Writers:** *Lois Kibbee, Eric Rubinton*

Background

"*Edge of Night* is not a soap opera," insists Lois Kibbee, who plays the imperious Geraldine Saxon on the show; "it's a mystery-melodrama"—albeit with a strong infusion of sex and star-crossed romance. That of course makes it different from the other daytime dramas, which are sex and star-crossed romance with a strong infusion of mystery-melodrama. However you define *Edge*, its ability to evoke both sighs and gasps (often in the same breath) has helped keep it on the air for twenty-seven years. Much credit is due Henry Slesar, head writer from 1967 until this year, when he was succeeded by Lee Sheldon. And the tempestuous love stories, involving Sky and Raven, Preacher and Jody, are woven so well into the melodrama that the town of Monticello has become a major attraction in the emotional geography of daytime TV.

The Story

Sky and Raven are in love; but in order to spy on Ian Devereaux and worm secrets out of him, Raven has to pretend there's nothing between her and Sky. She even accepts Ian's invitation to go on a Caribbean weekend, although with misgivings. Ian proposes to her, and at first she refuses. Then, realizing that Sky will be arrested as a traitor if she doesn't learn Ian's secrets, she finally accepts the proposal.

Nora maliciously burns down the Tavern, but instead of fleeing the arson charge offers to sell some information she has to Nicole—for $25,000. Nicole agrees, and arranges a midnight meeting at WMON so that Nora can be recorded on videotape, especially Nora's admission that she had falsely accused Miles of attempting to rape her. Jody learns about the meeting and tells Gavin, who goes out to the studio in time to see Nicole rushing out to the parking lot. Inside, Gavin finds Nora's strangled body. Later Nicole confesses to the murder, apparently to protect her drunken husband, Miles.

Although engaged to Ian, Raven can't keep away from Sky. Ian catches them together and calls off the wedding—ruining her CEA spy plans. But David Cameron finds a way of salvaging the scheme. Raven "saves" Ian's life and "kills" his assailant, Snell. It's all a CEA subterfuge but it succeeds in getting Ian to trust Raven again. He proposes again, and again she reluctantly accepts. To convince him that the romance with Sky is really off, Sky proposes to Valerie. On Raven's wedding day, tears stream down her face.

Love may make the rest of the world go round, but it's espionage that sets romance spinning in Monticello. Raven must feign affection for Ian to protect her true love, Sky.

Raven and Sky must keep their passions in check, lest her CEA spy plans be ruined.

He may look a bit suspicious, but Preacher didn't do it. It was Nora who beat Barbara so brutally.

It turns out Preacher wasn't the one who brutally beat Barbara; it was Nora. And Miles wasn't the one who killed Nora; it was Cameron. And now Cameron sneaks up on Patricia and strangles her, nasty double agent that he is. Next, Cameron disguises himself and shoots Ian, who luckily is wearing a bullet-proof vest.

Finally, it is Raven who finds the CEA phone book of foreign agents: it's in Jeff Brown's diary and is written in chess notation. She programs the computer with this information, then goes to tell Cameron about it. He drugs her, takes her to a seemingly abandoned warehouse where CEA operative Richard Scanlon (aka Constantine) struggles to save her. Cameron strangles him.

Cameron soon gets his come-uppance, however, when Sky invites him to press the key that will bring the CEA list up on the display terminal. The machine's been rigged to electrocute whoever touches it, and Cameron goes up in smoke.

Raven's and Ian's marriage, it turns out, was a hoax (an actor performed it instead of a minister), so Raven is free to marry Sky. Their wedding day is marred by the revelation that Sky is broke—Spencer has converted all the money into diamonds and has fled with Camilla! Camilla eventually turns up, but *sans* diamonds. If Sky and Raven can find a mysterious limping man, they may get some answers.

Only on the Soaps does a wedding turn out to be a hoax. Ian and Raven's marriage was "performed" by an actor, so she is free to marry Sky.

Jody and Preacher are in love, but his ne'er-do-well father, Del, shows up to spoil things. Then another murder: Miles's wife Nicole dies during her first newscast. Someone has poisoned her make-up with pesticide. And the make-up lady's husband has a limp—hmmm.

Life in Monticello gets even more dangerous when somebody tries to kill Preacher and a hood tries to kidnap Jody (Miles saves her). And when the ruby that Del filched turns up in Jody's theatrical headdress during a play, a mysterious underworld character named Sully shows up to grab it. The gem, though, is fake, so Sully has one of his henchmen hold Jody and Preacher hostage. Preacher manages to escape. Soon Sully himself is shot, and Stan Hathaway is tricked into confessing to Nicole's murder.

There's a new low-rent, high-tech office building called the Isis Building, and soon the high-class tenants start developing a collective paranoia. Perhaps most disturbed of all is a high-level executive of UnaNet, who plunges to his death from Isis's twenty-sixth floor. Then Didi (another tenant) has a nervous breakdown and is taken to the hospital. To investigate, Sky and Raven rent an office in the building,

his

posing as owners of a video dating service. They learn that both Isis and UnaNet are owned by Alicia "Grantman" (actually Van Dine), a former lover and nemesis of Sky's and one of the wealthiest women in the world. She and her younger brother Louis—a man who walks with a limp—occupy the two top floors of the building.

Mike Karr, smeared by false allegations, nevertheless mounts an independent campaign for district attorney—backed by the redoubtable Geraldine Saxon.

And poor Preacher. His love, Jody, seems to have fallen under the spell of a handsome young Svengali named Robbie Hamlin, who runs the Video Disco. The nightspot is being investigated in connection with the robbery of electronic equipment. Despite his initial fits of jealousy, Preacher begins to sense that Jody is under some sinister influence. Davey Oakes and Davey's mother seem equally under Robbie's control.

Miles is just beginning to recover from the death of Nicole some months earlier. While away in Fair River, far from Monticello, Miles pours out his grief to Chris, who comforts him so well that they end up in bed together. Back in town, Chris's lover, Derek, begins to suspect that she is having an affair with Miles. On his return to Monticello, Miles soon admits that it's true.

Mike Carr is the victim of a smear campaign when he runs for district attorney, but with the support of his wife, Nancy, he refuses to back down.

A mysterious electronic voice in the Isis building orders a henchman to "neutralize" Cliff, who knows too much. The henchman pipes gas into Cliff's apartment but at the last minute Cliff is saved by the chance arrival of Preacher and Mitzi.

In an effort to learn the nature of the hold Robbie has over Jody, Dr. Beth Corell tries unsuccessfully to hypnotize the girl. All Jody can say is, "Robbie knows what's best for me." After two thugs beat up Preacher, he barges into the Video Disco to confront Robbie, who he knows is responsible. But Jody screams at Preacher to get out. Devastated, Preacher leaves.

Later, Robbie overhears another suspicious character calling the police and saying he's got some evidence about Hamlin. The informer is found murdered in Preacher's apartment.

Cliff tries to explore the upper floors of the Isis Building. Chased by unknown assailants, he ends up trapped in a stark white room on the thirtieth floor. He discovers that Louis is the evil creature behind the electronic voice. Using a "Multi-Wave Color Signal Generator," Louis is able to flash subliminal messages on TV screens, thus manipulating Robbie Hamlin and ultimately all of Monticello's residents.

Jody has just been programmed to murder Preacher at the Video Disco. Miles and Chris show up in time to see Jody aiming the gun at her lover. Preacher moves closer, telling Jody how much he loves her. Trembling, Jody cocks the gun but at the last instant fires all the bullets into the disco's video screen and collapses in Preacher's arms.

Realizing he's in a tight spot, Louis orders his henchmen to eliminate the Whitneys, Geraldine, Preacher, and Miles. As an afterthought, he says, "Add Robbie Hamlin to that list."

Robbie decides to get out of town. He chloroforms Jody, but before he can kidnap her Preacher arrives and the two men fight it out. An explosion sets the screen on fire and soon the whole building is in flames. Preacher knocks Robbie out and drags him from the building, but he doesn't realize that Jody is locked in the back room. Ultimately, he does rescue her. Meanwhile, Miles, Derek, Sky, and Gunther helicopter to the roof of the Isis Building and there effect the rescue of Cliff, Mitzi, and Alicia, all of whom had been subjected to mental torture by the evil Louis. Louis is arrested and Sky realizes that Alicia did not know about her brother's plots.

Mike Karr wins the election for D.A., Preacher is reunited with Jody, and Raven and Sky are given detective licenses. But of course, despite the dramatic story wrap-up, the soap must go on; and so soon Raven and Sky are investigating the "haunted" Whitney Mansion. It turns out it's Spencer Varney who's haunting the place; he's looking for the diamonds he stole from Sky and Raven. Then Chris's apartment is robbed of a box of photos showing her son Matthew and her dead husband Walter. Also, Jody and Preacher can't be left in bliss. Jody tells her lover that she may go off to college. (In fact, Lori Loughlin, who plays Jody, decided to leave the soap by the end of the year.) Chris, alas, is still torn between Derek and Miles.

Profiles

Forrest Compton
(Mike Karr)

Forrest Compton had already made a solid name for himself in Hollywood, in such movies as *Inherit the Wind*, *The Children's Hour*, and *The Outsider*, before joining *Edge* in June 1971. He's also a known quantity in nighttime television, having appeared in numerous episodes of *Gomer Pyle—USMC*, *Hogan's Heroes*, *The Fugitive*, *Mayberry, R.F.D.*, and others. Compton has done an impressive amount of stage work as well, recently appearing with Betsy Palmer in *Sandcastles*, at the Westport, (Connecticut) Country Playhouse. A Pennsylvania boy, he graduated from Swarthmore College and went on to an M.F.A. degree at Yale Drama School. He and his wife Jeanne divide their time between their Manhattan apartment and their home on Shelter Island.

Joel Crothers
(Dr. Miles Cavanaugh)

Now in his early forties and as dashing as ever, Joel Crothers made his Broadway debut at age twelve, in *The Remarkable Mr. Pennypacker*, with Burgess Meredith. While still a schoolboy at Birch Wathen in Manhattan, he made TV appearances in prime-time anthologies such as *Studio One*, *Playhouse 90*, and *Kraft Theatre*. After a Harvard education and a number of Hollywood westerns, Joel moved into daytime serials: *Dark Shadows*, *The Secret Storm*, *Somerset Five*, and (in the spring of 1977) *The Edge of Night*.

Charles Flohe
(John Willard "Preacher" Emerson)

The man is blessed. After graduating from Seton Hall in New Jersey, Charles Flohe came to New York City and picked up first prize in an international modeling competition at the Waldorf Astoria. For the next two years his piercing blue eyes flashed from the pages of *Gentlemen's Quarterly* and *Cosmopolitan*, among others. In 1980 he decided to study acting, and on his twenty-fifth birthday, November 29, 1982, he auditioned for the part of Preacher, his first major role.

Ann Flood
(Nancy Karr)

A twenty-two-year veteran of *Edge*, Ann Flood was nominated for an Emmy in 1981–82 as outstanding actress in a daytime drama. This Long Island native made her first Broadway appearance in *Kismet* in 1954, when she was about twenty-two. After a number of television shows and forays to Hollywood, Ms. Flood settled in Manhattan where she married Herbert A. Granath, now the president of ABC Video Enterprises. They have four children, Kevin Michael, Brian John, Peter James, and Karen.

David Froman
(Gunther Wagner)

David Froman, whose father was chief of the Peoria Indian tribe from 1947 to 1976, was born in Oklahoma. After receiving a B.A. degree from the University of Denver and a master's degree in theater from the University of Kansas, he taught in the public school system and in several universities. Eight years of that was enough and in 1981 he got his first break as a professional actor: the lead in a dinner theater production of *The King and I.* That fall, David landed the role of the menacing, street-wise Gunther Wagner, Sky Whitney's chauffeur on *Edge.* He and his wife Audrey and two daughters live in Staten Island, New York.

Sharon Gabet
(Raven Whitney)

When not playing the spoiled, vengeful, multiply-married Raven Whitney, Sharon Gabet jumps out of airplanes and heads up a rock-and-roll band called Raven. She had done some college theater (at Cornell) and off-Broadway work before landing her role on *Edge* in 1980; but perhaps equally important to her development as an actress were her experiences working in hospitals. She graduated from Purdue University with a degree in nursing, and worked in several medical facilities, including a coronary care unit in Harlem. "Seeing people with their defenses down," she says, gave her insights into human nature which she might not otherwise have had.

Lois Kibbee
(Geraldine Whitney Saxon)

A fourteen-year veteran of *Edge*, Lois Kibbee belongs to the third generation of an acting family which spans the last hundred years. Now in her sixties, Ms. Kibbee has been acting since the age of five and has appeared in over three hundred stage productions, playing roles from Lady Macbeth to Auntie Mame. She's also produced and directed scores of plays, including a touring production of *The Prime of Miss Jean Brodie*, starring Kathryn Crosby. Lois Kibbee has written biographies of Christine Jorgenson and Joan Bennett, and for the past few years has been an associate writer for *Edge*.

Larkin Malloy
(Schuyler "Sky" Whitney)

When Larkin Malloy assumed the role of Sky in 1980, the character was an archvillain; but he has evolved into an heroic figure now. For that kind of transition, you need acting, and Malloy has honed his craft in many regional theater productions, several at Minneapolis's famed Tyrone Guthrie Theatre. A native New Yorker, he has appeared in off-off-Broadway productions (e.g., *Cyrano de Bergerac* and *The Taming of the Shrew*). Like his costar, Charles Flohe, Malloy is an excellent fencer.

Arrivals and Departures

Willie Aames
(Robbie Hamlin)

At twenty-two, Willie Aames is an old-timer on TV, having played Tommy Bradford for five years on *Eight Is Enough*. He still has a recurring role on *Love Boat* and has completed a pilot for Aaron Spelling Productions called *Tom Swift*. In fact, the word is that young Aames has never gone more than a month without work (as either an actor or musician) since the fourth grade. He's even done two movies: the critically savaged *Paradise*, and the light-weight *Zapped* (with Scott Baio). The role of Robbie (initiated this summer) is thought of as a short-term character, but in soaps one never knows.

Lori Loughlin
(Jody Travis)

Before joining *Edge* in 1980, at the age of fifteen, Lori had already had six years' experience as a model and an actress in TV commercials. She'd also appeared in the TV movie, *Too Far to Go*, with Blythe Danner and Michael Moriarty. Still a teenager, Lori has completed a pilot for Aaron Spelling and acted a part in the movie, *Amityville 3D*. She attends drama and voice classes and models for the Elite Agency. Lori still lives with her parents and younger brother, Roy, on Long Island.

Lisa Sloan
(Nicole Cavanaugh)

Alas, Nicole was killed off during the summer, victim of the needs of melodrama. The tall, blue-eyed Kentucky-born actress who played her is alive and well in New York City, however. Lisa Sloan has appeared on Broadway in the long-running *Gemini* and is a founding member of the American Repertory Theatre in Boston, where she played Helena in *A Midsummer Night's Dream*. She has also appeared in several films, including *Starting Over*.

Jennifer Taylor
(Chris Egan)

Paris-born Jennifer Taylor joined *Edge* in May 1983, as policewoman Chris Egan—a part she trained for by taking karate lessons. Before this part Jennifer played the role of Barbara on *All My Children*. She has also done a lot of regional theater, including productions of *The Children's Hour* and *Our Town*. She is married and lives in Brooklyn.

General Hospital

ABC

The Cast

Denise
Alexander...... *Dr. Lesley Webber*
Rachel Ames ..... *Audrey Hobart*
Kabir Bedi
(temporary
role) .... *Lord Rama*
Sam Behrens...... *Jake Meyer*
John
Beradino .... *Dr. Steve Hardy*
Loanne
Bishop .... *Rose Kelly*
Steve Bond........ *Jimmy Lee Holt*
Susan Brown ...... *Dr. Gail Adamson*
Gail Rae Carlson
(left in
spring) .... *Susan Moore*
Leslie
Charleson...... *Dr. Monica Quartermaine*
Brian Patrick
Clarke (started
this year)....... *Dr. Grant Putnam*
Booth
Colman .... *Dr. Hector Jerrold*
Norma
Connolly .... *Ruby Anderson*
Melinda
Cordell........ *Natalie Dearborn*
Stuart
Damon .... *Dr. Alan Quartermaine*
Todd Davis........ *Bryan Phillips*
Lieux
Dressler .... *Alice Grant*
Genie Francis
(temporary
return).......... *Laura Baldwin Spencer*
Anthony Geary
(left late in
year) .... *Luke Spencer*
Gerold
Gordon........ *Dr. Mark Dante*
David Groh .... *Donald Lewis Brock*
Peter Hansen ..... *Lee Baldwin*

Wiley Harker
(joined and left
in spring)....... *Crane Tolliver*
Bob Hastings...... *Capt. Ramsey*
Shell Kepler....... *Amy Vining*
Joe Lambie
(temporary
role) .... *Gregory Malko*
Anna Lee......... *Lila Quartermaine*
Roberta Leighton
(started in
summer)........ *Shirley Pickett*
David Lewis....... *Edward Quartermaine*
John Martinuzzi
(came and left
in fall) .... *Stavros Cassadine*
Robin Mattson
(left in
midyear)....... *Heather Webber*
Frank
Maxwell........ *Dan Rooney*
Jeanna
Michaels .... *Constance Townley*
Demi Moore ...... *Jackie Templeton*
Chris
Robinson....... *Dr. Rick Webber*
Tristan
Rogers .... *Robert Scorpio*
Merri Lynn
Ross .... *Emma Lutz*
Emma
Samms .... *Holly Sutton*
Kin Shriner (left
toward end of
year) .... *Scotty Baldwin*
Rick Springfield
(left in
spring) .... *Noah Drake*
John Stamos...... *Blackie Parrish*
Danielle von
Zerneck (joined
early in
year) .... *Louisa (Lou) Swenson*
Sherilyn
Wolter .... *Celia Quartermaine*
Sharon Wyatt ..... *Tiffany Hill*
Jacklyn
Zeman.......... *Bobbie Spencer, R.N.*

Executive
Producer: *Gloria Monty*
Associate
Producer: *Gerald M. Jaskulski*
Directors: *Phil Sogard, Marlena Laird, Alan Pultz*
Production
Consultant: *Jerry Balme*
Head
Writer: *Anne Howard Bailey*

Background

Necessity is the mother of invention; and in the case of *General Hospital*, the threat of cancellation was the mother of an upward surge in ratings. And Gloria Monty, the executive producer brought in to save the show in 1978, is generally conceded to be the toughest mother of all.

General Hospital started out promisingly enough in 1963 as a modest hospital saga capitalizing on the nighttime popularity of *Dr. Kildare* and *Ben Casey*. NBC was launching *The Doctors* at the same time. Jim Young, *GH*'s first producer/director, had a pitifully small budget to work with for the first few years, but some shrewd character delineation by writers Frank and Doris Hursley soon drew viewers into the lives and problems of nurse Jessie Brewer and Dr. Steve Hardy and the others. Within five years after launch, the show had risen to the top of the daytime ratings, had changed from black-and-white to color (1966), and had gone from a half hour to forty-five minutes.

It was a good show, but with changes in writers and directors it seemed to have lost its original impetus; some say it had played out most of the possibilities of its limited premise. In the mid-seventies, the ratings dropoff was becoming serious, and in 1977, *GH*'s share of the audience fell to 16 percent. Cancellation seemed imminent.

Then several things happened. Jacqueline Smith, ABC's new head of daytime programming, made the decision to try more youthful storylines. Gloria Monty came aboard as producer on January 1, 1978, and expressed her determination to speed up the pacing. And young Douglas Marland was hired as head writer at the urging of Agnes Nixon. He quickly came up with a prominent storyline for the teenage characters, Scotty Baldwin and Laura Vining. He also created a sensational character in student nurse Bobbie Spencer (played by Jackie Zeman), who connived viciously to steal Scotty from Laura. That summer the ratings doubled, as an increasingly large teenage audience tuned in.

Then Gloria Monty hired a highly kinetic actor named Anthony Geary to play Bobbie Spencer's underworld brother, Luke. It soon became apparent that every time Luke came anywhere near Laura there'd be an upward blip in the ratings. Pat Falken Smith (taking over as head writer from Doug Marland) undertook to write the now famous, or infamous, rape scene in which Laura, the wholesome but ambivalent teenager, succumbs to the lustful force of Luke Spencer.

"At the time that we did that scene we didn't really know that Luke and Laura would have such charisma," said Genie Francis recently. "And I don't think the writers sat down and said, 'I know, let's have a story where the guy rapes the girl and she falls in love with him.' I don't think that's what they were doing at all."

Nevertheless, that's exactly what happened, and the ratings went through the roof. When Luke and Laura were finally married, an estimated sixteen million Americans watched. It was the largest audience in the history of soap opera.

Other experiments seemed to work equally well. The introduction of celebrity drop-in characters (notably Elizabeth Taylor, Richard Simmons, and Rick Springfield) helped pump up viewership. Nor did it hurt when the plot turned to melodramatic adventure á la *Dr. No*, and swept the characters off to tropical islands for far-flung exploits. Soon other soaps were scrambling to follow suit.

But always the action would return to the fictive harbor town of Port Charles, with new characters like Scorpio and the beautiful Holly mingling destinies with the powerful Quartermaine family, the maverick Spencers, the Baldwins, and the Webbers.

There'll be one Spencer missing in 1984, and his absence will be felt for some time. On December 12, 1983, Tony Geary announced in a press conference at New York's Plaza Hotel that he was leaving the show. "I do consider Luke Spencer the Hamlet of daytime," he said, ". . . because there were no boundaries on the man." Leaving the show, however, afforded Geary the chance to play a real Shakespearean role, that of Octavius Caesar in *Antony and Cleopatra*. Quite simply, he says, "Luke Spencer has been done" and it's time to move on to other roles.

He did, however, emphasize that "Luke Spencer lives on and more than likely will be returning from time to time," although not for a major storyline or long-term involvement. As for the Luke-and-Laura chemistry, Geary feels it's evolved into a Tony-and-Genie acting chemistry and could be transferred to some other set of characters, perhaps in a play or film. "It would be very exciting working with Genie" on other projects, he says. Whether the American public can accept those two actors as, say, Hamlet and Ophelia, or Stanley Kowalski and Blanche DuBois, is another question. For millions of soap fans, Tony and Genie will be Luke and Laura forever.

The Story

Talk about banging your head against the wall. Susan has totalled the car and seems at death's door. Scotty Baldwin, wangling for control of her money, marries her in the hospital. In short order he pulls half a million from Susan's son's trust fund to invest in a mall.

Noah and Tiffany are having problems—she's jealous of his friendship with Bobbie Spencer, and with good reason; before long Bobbie and Noah head for the bedroom.

Holly has her hands full. She's pregnant with Luke's child, she thinks he's dead, and she's about to be deported. Marriage to Scorpio offers a solution.

Then comes the tragic news: Luke has disappeared in the mountains. In fact, he's been practically killed by an avalanche and is paralyzed from the waist down. Holly and Robert fly out to the morgue to view the avalanche victims, and one of them does seem to re-resemble Luke; then they see Luke's half a sixpence and are convinced the body is his.

Later, Holly finds she is pregnant with Luke's child. She tries to get a job, doesn't have the necessary "green card" and is about to be deported to England. Robert Scorpio, who loves her, convinces her to marry him—for the sake of the child.

Showing up at the Quartermaine house is a brash youngster named Jimmy Lee Holt, who claims (and later proves) that he is in fact Edward Q's illegitimate son.

He's not after money; but another stranger, the disreputable old Crane Tolliver, certainly is. He shows up at the now-recovered Susan's door, declaring there are no legitimate heirs to the Quartermaine money because he is Lila Q's only true, legal husband (long-ago divorce proceedings were never properly completed). Tolliver,

Suspicions swirl around Scotty when Susan is found murdered. He's booked before the real killer is discovered.

through Susan, demands two million dollars to disappear. Everyone has a reason to hate Susan: Scotty and Heather because Susan is exposing Scotty's scheme (including forgery) to get Susan's money; the Quartermaines because of Susan's blackmail demand. That night a shot rings out and Susan falls dead.

Blackie made his own transition from bad kid to good kid, and now he's helping Lou, the young runaway, to do the same.

Scorpio's life is complicated by the rekindling of feelings for an old love, Constance Townley.

Police Commissioner Robert Scorpio first suspects Alice Grant, to whom Susan leaves everything. Later he books a more likely suspect, Scotty Baldwin. Or is Heather trying to frame Scotty? She too is locked up on suspicion of murder. The real killer, it turns out, is Tolliver, who hired someone to dress like him and go to jail that night while Tolliver killed Susan. Perfect alibi, but Scorpio (using Heather as bait) traps him. Tolliver is shot and dies in the hospital.

Meanwhile Blackie, a bad kid gone good, finds himself hiding a runaway girl, Lou, from thugs. He cleans her up, and to disguise her, dresses her in Tiffany's clothes; before you can say Pygmalion he's fallen in love with her.

Things go less well for Holly, who miscarries Luke's baby. Meanwhile, out in the woods, Luke's paralyzed legs begin to develop feeling again. Holly's husband-of-convenience, Robert, also develops feelings, for old flame Constance Townley. But his real feelings are for his wife, Holly. Still in the backwoods, Luke progresses from crutches to walker, and sends his therapist, Natalie, into town to learn news of his friends, particularly Holly. Natalie learns about the marriage of Scorpio, but doesn't tell Luke.

Eventually, Holly begins to feel more loving toward her husband, but can't forget Luke. She makes a farewell hike into the woods, stares out at the lake, and tosses away Luke's half a sixpence. (In fact, she very nearly runs into him.) Returning to Port Charles, she gives herself to Scorpio, finally consummating their marriage. When Luke at last returns to town he knocks on Scorpio's door. He's told Robert is away, but "Mrs. Scorpio" is home. Holly appears at the top of the stairs. Luke, devastated, turns and flees.

Celia Quartermaine, engaged to Grant Putnam, lusts after Jimmy Lee Holt. She starts a sculpture of him, but the sittings quickly turn into a lying down affair. By the time Celia's affections swing away from Holt to Grant, Putnam's about ready to call the marriage off. He calls it on again when Natalie tells him it's an important component in an undercover operation. It appears there are spies and top-secret research in Port Charles. Shh.

Meanwhile, Blackie is urging the frightened runaway girl, Lou, to cooperate with Scorpio to convict deadly thugs Augie, Largo, and Hand. Augie kills Hand while burning down the clinic, and eventually he comes after Lou. She's saved at the last moment when Scorpio and Blackie kick down the door and shoot Augie.

Though torn up about Holly, Luke agrees to become Don Brock's partner in a new restaurant-casino, to be called "Luke's Place." And Heather opens a cafe on the waterfront. Jimmy Lee (with Quartermaine money) starts a construction company. Everybody's getting something out of this mall.

Natalie is really Natasha, who reports to Yuri, a higher-up spy, and Grant is the mole she controls. They plot to steal secret research information from Dr. Jerrold concerning a miniature power unit that could provide a limitless energy source. Intrigue mounts over this

Grant gets a little steamed when he learns of Celia's passion for Jimmy Lee.

"Prometheus disc" and Grant's contorted schemes to steal it. He fumbles the job and Luke ends up with the disc, unaware that it could explode. He keeps it in the heel of his shoe.

Luke runs for mayor, and his opponent is Lee Baldwin, whose son Scotty attacks Luke on TV as a "former mob stooge." But spies, not mobsters, are the problem these days. Spy Brenich tries to kill spy Connie (who's saved by Luke), and when spy Grant refuses to kill Celia or Dr. Jerrold, he himself ends up getting stung by a scorpion (he survives). When Dr. Jerrold is shot dead by another evil agent, Grant becomes the prime suspect.

Luke decides to check up on Natalie. He locates her previous husband and learns from him that she's a violent anti-American fanatic. Later, Grant invites the Scorpios out to an evening at the theater so that Natalie can sneak into their townhouse and search the communications room. Connie is there and jumps her. During the struggle a gun goes off and Natalie slumps to the floor, clutching her side. Of no more use to the spy ring, Natalie is soon murdered in the hospital.

Lesley has developed a wicked gambling problem and even

gambles away her husband Rick's paycheck. Lou begins worrying about Blackie's affections, or rather about the degree of his commitment to her. He doesn't feel ready for commitment yet—after all, they're both still kids. Bobbie would like to get some kind of commitment from D.L. (Donald Lewis) Brock, particularly now that she suspects that she's carrying his child. But just as she's getting ready to tell him she's pregnant, he talks about how kids take away one's freedom and tie one down.

Luke finally understands that his old nemesis, Robert Scorpio, is the only person he can trust with the Prometheus disc. Scorpio has been administering a lie detector test to Grant and has found him probably innocent of the various murders that have been taking place recently. But Robert still believes that Grant could lead him to the DVX's spymaster. Ultimately, in fact, this is what happens, but not before many nefarious twists and turns. Holly, Celia, and Luke, for instance, are held for ransom in exchange for Robert's half of the disc microfilm. Unfortunately, it's a fake. International bad guys do not like to be given fake goods, and so the order is given to ice Luke and Holly. Grant, however, is rapidly turning from a bad guy into a good guy, and he slips blanks into the guards' guns. In the barrage that follows, Grant, Luke, and Holly are all "shot." They're then rescued by Robert, who places Grant under arrest. Pleading for asylum in the U.S., Grant tells the authorities about the DVX's secret workings. He also makes possible the capture of several major foreign agents.

Except for Lesley's gambling problem, which continues to cause a strain, things work out pretty well all around: Luke is elected mayor of Port Charles; Grant is granted asylum and is united with his love, Celia; D.L. decides he'd like a child after all and proposes to Bobbie. Even Jake and Rose, who love each other but were kept from marrying because he is Jewish and she is not, come to realize that they can work out their religious differences.

It is into this uncharacteristically placid town that the long-lost but not forgotten Laura sets her well-turned foot. She has secretly followed Luke around, causing in him eerie feelings of premonition.

It seems Laura has had an eventful couple of years away from Port Charles. Helena Cassadine kidnapped her, then Stavros Cassadine became obsessed with her, kept her captive, and when she wouldn't become his mistress, married her (Laura had heard that Luke was dead and so didn't care what she did). Now Stavros has sworn revenge on Helena who, wanting Stavros for herself, arranged for Laura to escape from him. One of Stavros's thugs has been sent to recapture her during Luke's inauguration ceremony. He fails. Luke and Laura are reconciled and find themselves as deeply in love as ever. Stavros doesn't give up easily, though, and near the end of 1983 Luke kills him accidentally. The fearsome Helena decides to lift the dread Cassadine curse which she'd imposed on Luke and Laura's wedding day several years earlier; and it looks as though Luke and Laura will go off into soap nirvana. Dare one say "happily ever after?"

Profiles

Denise Alexander
(Dr. Lesley Webber)

A real *Wunderkind*, Denise Alexander worked regularly in TV all through high school and college, appearing on *I Remember Mama*, *Twilight Zone*, and many other shows. Still in her teens, she landed the role of Susan Martin in *Days of Our Lives* and stayed six years. A popular actress with daytime fans, she joined *General Hospital* in March 1972 and in 1977 received and Emmy nomination for her portrayal of Dr. Lesley Webber. She lives in Beverly Hills with numerous pets and has contributed recipes to the recently published *Love in the Afternoon Cookbook*.

Brian Patrick Clarke
(Dr. Grant Putnam)

The convoluted storyline of the mysterious Dr. Putnam dominated *GH* for much of 1983. A former Yale football star, Brian Clarke went professional for a season with the World Football League before heading for Los Angeles in 1976 to pursue an acting career. He began landing some TV roles in series, commercials, and TV movies before coming to *GH* in 1982.

Stuart Damon
(Dr. Alan Quartermaine)

Since becoming a regular on *General Hospital* in 1977, the soft-spoken Mr. Damon has been twice nominated for a daytime Emmy. He started out as a song-and-dance man, appearing in over fifty musicals including the Broadway production of *Irma La Douce*, where his dance partner was Elliot Gould. In 1964 he was named most promising performer by *Theatre World* for his part in *The Boys from Syracuse*; and the following year he starred with Leslie Ann Warren in the TV musical production of *Cinderella*. He is married to British-born actress Deirdre Ottewill-Damon; they have two children (Jennifer and Christopher) and a dog (Odette).

Demi Moore
(Jackie Templeton)

Demi Moore (nee Guynes) moved around a lot as a kid—about forty-eight times, she thinks, which meant attending forty-eight schools. While attending Walt Whitman High School in West Los Angeles she became interested in performing, moved out on her own (that would make forty-nine moves) and got herself an agent. At seventeen she started modeling, and at eighteen landed a couple of roles on television. Demi made several films and in February 1981 married song-writer and performer Freedy Moore. In December of that year she joined *General Hospital* as Jackie. She and Freddy live with cats and toy poodles in a West Hollywood apartment.

Tristan Rogers
(Robert Scorpio)

Australian-born actor Tristan Rogers has a wonderfully meaty part in Police Commissioner Robert Scorpio, and his dashing debut in 1980 won him *Soap Opera Digest*'s Soapy Award as most exciting new actor. After starring in an Australian police series, Rogers moved to Europe, where he appeared in many BBC productions. He moved to the United States in 1978 and worked at getting rid of his accent. But when ABC hired him he was told, "Keep the old accent." And he has, lacing Scorpio's dialogue with Australian colloquialisms.

Emma Samms
(Holly Sutton)

Another foreign touch is Emma Samms's lilting English accent. The strikingly beautiful young actress was born in a theatrical family in London, and from the age of two until six she performed intermittently with the Royal Ballet. Her education swerved from pre-med to modeling to acting and she was soon appearing in movies: *Arabian Adventure* and *More Wild, Wild West*, neither of which gave much indication of what she could do, or how completely she would soon capture the imagination of a huge daytime audience. Ms. Samms is a great success as a model, too, especially in Japan, where she is spokeswoman for a large cosmetics company. She joined *GH* in 1982.

John Stamos
(Blackie Parrish)

Still a teenager, John Stamos's 1982 debut on *General Hospital* was also his first appearance on television. Signed to appear in five episodes, he generated so much electricity that the role was continued indefinitely, leading to a 1983 Emmy nomination as best supporting actor in a soap. A California boy, John was always interested in puppetry and music and currently sings with his band, Bad Boyz.

Jacklyn Zeman
(Bobbie Spencer, R.N.)

The story goes that one evening, record promoter and public relations lady Jackie Zeman suddenly decided she wanted to be a soap opera actress. The next morning she enrolled in drama school and three months later made her debut on *One Life to Live*. After her character was killed off, she came to *General Hospital* in 1977. Impulsively, she left near the end of 1982. In May 1983, she began hosting the radio show, *Soap Talk*, on the ABC Radio Network.

Arrivals and Departures

Steve Bond
(Jimmy Lee Holt)

When handsome Steve Bond was in grade school, spirit, looks, and luck landed him a title part in the film, *Tarzan and the Jungle Boy*. The jungle boy made two sequels and several other films, including *The Arrangement* (playing Kirk Douglas's character as a boy), before throwing it over for rodeo riding. Steve broke horses, rode bulls, won trophies—and then got hurt. After recovering he went back to films, landed some TV roles, and in 1983 burst into soap stardom with the highly kinetic (indeed, lusty) character of Jimmy Lee Holt.

Genie Francis
(Laura Baldwin Spencer)

Genie Francis returned (temporarily) to *General Hospital* in November 1983, to recreate her famous role of Laura. Some sixteen million viewers (a daytime record) tuned in on November 16 and 17, 1981, when Laura married Luke Spencer. Genie left the show in January 1982 to pursue prime-time fame in *Bare Essence* and other high-paying but ill-fated projects. Although she'd vowed never to return to *GH*, millions of fans never doubted that she would one day set foot again in Port Charles.

Anthony Geary
(Luke Spencer)

Since joining *General Hospital* in 1978, Tony Geary's edgy portrayal of Luke Spencer has made him, by many accounts, the most popular actor on daytime television. Having grown up in Coalville, Utah, Geary was snatched from obscurity when Jack Albertson saw him perform in a play at the University of Utah and cast him in a touring production of *The Subject Was Roses*. Over forty stage productions followed and more than fifty television shows, including *Starsky & Hutch* and *All in the Family*. He won the 1981 Emmy Award as outstanding actor in daytime drama, and in 1982 he inaugurated a nightclub act—singing and dancing, the whole thing. Although he is one of the highest paid soap actors, Geary decided, "for my own personal growth," to leave the show at the end of 1983. His last episodes were taped on December 5th.

Robin Mattson
(Heather Webber)

Fans will miss Robin Mattson's Heather, who is being shipped off to Nevada for the forseeable future. Apparently the character's being written out of the show for now because Miss Mattson wants to make a stab at feature films and prime-time TV. She's played Heather since September 1980, and won *Soap Opera Digest*'s 1982–83 "Soapy" Award as daytime's favorite villainess. She was also nominated that year for an Emmy.

A child actress, Robin appeared at age nine in *Namu, the Killer Whale*, and later continued in the same vein in *Flipper* and *Gentle Ben*. Soon she was playing in various TV shows from *Charlie's Angels* to *The Incredible Hulk*. After graduating from Santa Monica City College, Robin continued studying psychology and has become a spokesperson for the National Mental Health Association. She recently received their Distinguished Service Award.

Kin Shriner
(Scotty Baldwin)

Alas, by the end of 1983 that scheming manipulator, Scotty Baldwin, was no longer stirring up trouble in Port Charles, and the town will be duller without him. Kin had played Scotty once before on *GH*, from 1977 to 1980, at which time he left for another soap, NBC's short-lived *Texas*. When *Texas* folded, Kin returned, but instead of the concerned, clean-cut Scotty of the past, there was now a money-hungry conniver—a much more exciting part to play. Son of comedian Herb Shriner, Kin made his television debut in *The Young and the Restless*, then went on to *Rich Man, Poor Man* and many other roles. Kin's twin brother, Wil, is a comedian, and his sister Indy is an actress.

Danielle von Zerneck
(Louise [Lou] Swenson)

Danielle, the teenage daughter of film producer Frank von Zerneck, spent her early years in New York before moving to North Hollywood. She appeared in three TV movies, all produced by her father: *Sharon: Portrait of a Mistress*, *The Love Canal*, and *In the Custody of Strangers*. She lives in Los Angeles with her parents and her younger brother, Francis, and aspires to perform on Broadway.

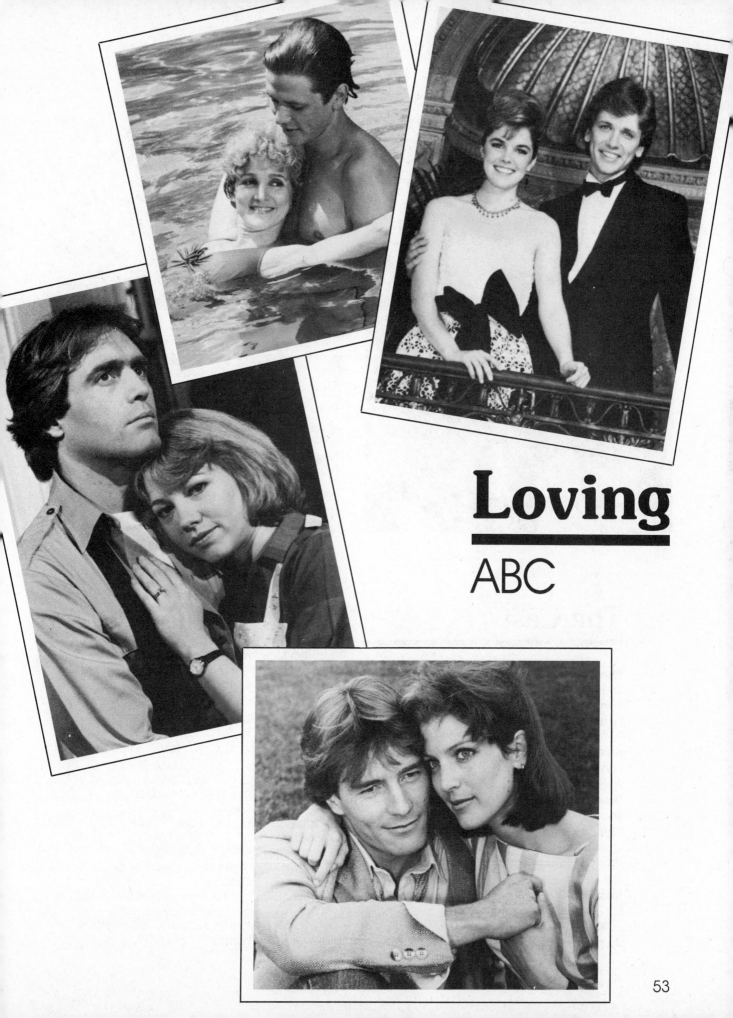

Loving

ABC

The Cast

Wesley Addy .... *Cabot Alden*
Jennifer Ashe .... *Lily Slater*
Pamela Blair .... *Rita Mae Bristow*
Peter Brown (took over in
    fall) .... *Roger Forbes*
Bryan Cranston .... *Douglas Donovan*
John Cunningham .... *Garth Slater*
Augusta Dabney .... *Isabelle Alden*
Peter Davies .... *Father Jim Vochek*
Shannon Eubanks .... *Ann Alden Forbes*
Anthony Herrera (new in
    late fall) .... *Dane Hammond*
Patricia Kalember .... *Merrill Vochek*
Teri Keane .... *Rose Donovan*
Noah Keen .... *Patrick Donovan*
Susan Keith (new in late
    fall) .... *Shana*
James Kiberd .... *Mike Donovan*

Tom Ligon .... *Billy Bristow*
Christopher
    Marcantel .... *Curtis Alden*
Marilyn McIntyre .... *Noreen Vochek*
                              Donovan
John Shearin (left at end
    of summer) .... *Roger Forbes*
Perry Stephens .... *Jack Forbes*
Lauren-Marie Taylor ...... *Stacey Donovan*
Susan Walters .... *Lorna Forbes*
Ann Williams .... *June Slater*

Created by: *Agnes Nixon and Douglas*
                Marland
Producer: *Joseph Stuart*
Associate
Producer: *Barbara Duggan*
Directors: *Robert Scinto, Andrew D.*
                Weyman
Writers: *Douglas Marland (head writer),*
              Patric Mulcahey, Nancy
              Franklin, Kathleen Lawlor, Percy
              Granger

Background

A bouncing brand-new soap opera has come to ABC, the first such arrival in eight years, and its parentage is impressive: Agnes Nixon (creator and/or one-time head writer of most of the soaps now on the air) and Douglas Marland, three-time Emmy winner for best writing in daytime TV. Whether *Loving* lasts is hard to predict—it's not easy to win people over to a new soap—but ABC has guaranteed to keep it on the air at least two years.

A contemporary drama set in the university town of Corinth, *Loving* involves the students and administration of mythical Alden University, as well as a number of local residents. The Forbes family, the Vocheks, the Donovans, and the Aldens dominate the cast.

The first episode aired June 27, 1983, the morning after a two-hour ABC-TV movie of the same name.

The Story

The pilot movie revealed the existence of a prostitution ring in Corinth which uses young college girls. TV newswoman Merrill Vochek finds out about it and tries to solve the murder of one of the college girls, which the police are ignoring. In love with Doug Donovan, a drama professor at Alden University, Merrill finds herself powerfully attracted to the dashing Kennedy-esque university president, Roger Forbes, who has just promised his wife that he'd be faithful to her. The pilot ends with the murder solved, the prostitution ring smashed, and Merrill's honor intact. Just.

But as the daily serial begins, we see that Merrill and Roger are still strongly attracted to each other. They end up in a hunting cabin in a rainstorm and fall into a passionate embrace. Meanwhile Curtis Alden and Lorna (Roger's daughter) are heading out to the cabin. Roger's wife Ann telephones the cabin, and, with the romantic spell broken, Roger and Merrill head back to town. When Curtis and Lorna arrive the cabin is empty, save for a mysterious scent of perfume.

The Slaters have problems: Garth's wife, Ann, is an alcoholic; Lily (their daughter) is terrified of her bullying and manipulative father

Merrill Vochek and Doug Donovan are in love, but how long will it be before he learns of her fated affair with Roger Forbes?

Roger has promised Ann that he'll be faithful to her, a promise that he'll be unable to keep.

and has recurrent nightmares involving him. Both Curtis and Jack (Roger's adopted son) are interested in Lily, but Jack's persistence and sensitivity eventually win her heart.

Mike Donovan is also having recurrent nightmares, but his are about Vietnam. Although his patient wife Noreen (Merrill's sister) wants

Lorna is putting the arm on Jack, but it's Lily who will steal his heart.

children, Mike turns sullen at the suggestion. Why bring kids into this lousy world?

Roger and Merrill try to break off their dangerous affair, but his trouble-making daughter, Lorna, makes sure they run into each other. Also Merrill has to interview Roger for a nationally syndicated series. At the Founder's Day picnic Roger grabs and kisses Merrill; she breaks free and runs straight into Doug's arms and, to his delight, agrees to be his wife.

Slutty Rita Mae tries to trap Jack but settles for Curtis in the bathhouse. Afterwards, she worries her husband Billy may find out and is stunned to realize her rings have disappeared. Voyeuristic Lorna has taken them. Curtis retrieves them and gets revenge on Jack by dressing up like him and pawning the rings. Rita Mae is furious at Jack until he collars Curtis and forces him to confess his chicanery.

Garth continues to manipulate his daughter Lily, and when she wins a statewide piano competition he tries to force her to come home early from the celebration party. But she's strong enough to refuse to leave. Garth is also a sneak; when he hears that Roger Forbes is seeing another woman, he plots to find out who it is.

Merrill and Roger find themselves together in New York—he's there to give a speech and she's there to cover it. When a blackout hits Manhattan the pair is trapped on the forty-seventh floor of the hotel. They light candles and are unable to resist making love. Doug shows up unexpectedly but is not suspicious. Roger and Merrill, though,

The Donovan clan is patient, but nothing seems to ease Mike's pain.

don't like to lie and skulk about; Roger plans to divorce Ann and Merrill can break off with Doug.

Later, back home in Corinth, she tries to think of a way of letting Doug down softly. She doesn't have a chance before Doug takes her to a surprise wedding shower. A stunned Merrill is subdued and leaves early. Finally she tells Doug she can't marry him because of her career as a TV newswoman. Furious, Doug goes out and gets himself drunk. Brought back home, Doug reaches out to Lorna and, thinking she's Merrill, kisses her passionately.

June is trying to quit drinking, and trying as well to get her wretched

Lorna Forbes is looking every inch the conniving little vixen she is.

husband Garth to stop bullying Lily. She threatens to tell Lily about Garth's penchant for wife-beating. When Lily arrives home, she finds her mother propped against a chair. Garth says June has been drinking again and fell down—hence the bruises.

Garth also blackmails Lily into breaking off with Jack. She resists the pressure, but when Garth threatens to send June away, Lily gives in, writing a tearful "Dear John" letter to Jack. But then she learns that her high school teachers had recommended that she skip her senior year and enroll at Alden University in the fall. Garth had known this

Rita Mae puts her best moves on Jack. Fortunately her best isn't enough to win him over.

and never told his daughter about it. She's outraged at his behavior and at his lame excuses (which turn out to be lies). Through it all, Jack sticks by her.

Alone with Noreen, Merrill tells her sister the truth about her love for Roger Forbes. Though at first taken aback, Noreen urges Merrill to follow her heart.

Lorna gets into hot water at a frat party and the next day she has a violently abusive argument with her mother Ann, even screaming that she hates her and everything she stands for. Roger had planned to ask Ann for a divorce that night, but seeing her so distraught he decides to put it off.

Jack confesses to Father Jim his growing suspicion that Lily is being abused—either beaten or sexually molested—by her father, Garth. But he has no proof. Lily meanwhile is beginning to manifest the effects of longterm abuse: she's developed a frightening, sluttish alter ego that tries to take over her personality. At last perceiving that Jack is her only hope for a normal life, she begs him to take her away where her father can't find her. Impulsively, he packs some things and they run off together.

While staying in a little town called Harper Falls, Jack earns some money at a stone quarry. But Lily's second personality comes slyly

Merrill and Roger fight to contain their passion for one another, but the fates seem determined to draw them together.

out and she gets herself up in a flashy red dress and picks up some guy to go dancing with. When Jack gets home she's already asleep. The next night she does it again, and Jack finds her burning with a fever. He drives straight to Corinth Hospital, where Lily's illness is diagnosed as meningitis.

When Garth shows up at the hospital, Jack very nearly slugs him. Later, Garth goes home and takes out his gun. As Lily gradually recovers, personalities one and two begin once again to alternately control her.

Noreen is having problems of her own with Mike, who refuses to seek psychiatric help for his Vietnam-induced recurrent nightmares, and who continues to reject the idea of having kids. Finally Noreen leaves him and moves in with her sister.

It finally homes in on Doug that Merrill is having an affair with Roger Forbes. Humiliated and angry he seeks out the comfortable company of Rita Mae. Lorna tells Cabot that her dad is having an affair with Merrill. Cabot's response is immediate: He orders Merrill to be fired from the TV station and blackballed in the industry!

Lorna (the little witch!) tries to seduce her professor, Doug, and though her direct approach—plunking herself in his bed—doesn't work, she's sure she'll get him eventually. First, she needs to get Rita Mae out of the way, and to that end writes to Billy that something's going wrong between Rita Mae and Professor Donovan. This leads to an awful fight between Billy and Rita Mae, culminating in Billy vowing to get a divorce.

During the scenes showing Billy trying to live on his own, *Loving* breaks one of the great soap opera taboos: showing housework. Billy can't seem to get the hang of laundry, and his cooking isn't so hot. Rita Mae, where are you?

Finally, tipped off about her husband's affair, Ann Forbes confronts Merrill, who apologizes for the pain she's caused. Ann tells her that her husband has had a string of affairs and that his real love is politics, not women.

Speeding away afterwards, the tearful Ann is stopped by a police car. Mike, the cop in charge, drives Ann home, but she's so upset that they stop at the pool house to talk awhile. Mike tells her that she's as brave as she is beautiful, and before you know it, the two of them are in each other's arms. It's their first experience with infidelity and it feels so good that they do it again the next day. By then Ann has confronted Roger and told him to pack up and get out.

Merrill gets increasingly disillusioned with Roger, first when he doesn't call and then when he wants to delay divorcing Ann until after the January election. (He's in line for Senator North's seat.) Merrill decides to break off the relationship.

June warns Jack that her husband Garth plans to prosecute him for "abducting" his daughter, Lily. Lily, meanwhile, recuperating at home, takes the gun from her father's desk drawer. As she hides in the bedroom, Garth stands in the doorway.

Sometime that night Garth attempts to rape Lily; soon afterwards he is shot and mortally wounded. Lily fainted when her father assaulted her, so she did not see who fired the shot. Hovering near death, the old reprobate gasps that Jack was the one who shot him. Jack is arrested; but Ann, who is also a suspect, is forced to admit that Roger had threatened to kill Garth. Then Merrill has to pipe up and say, no, Roger was with her at the time of the shooting. Finally, Lily says that *she* was the one who killed Garth. But some people think she's just protecting Jack. Into the midst of this lethal confusion steps a new character, Dane Hammond (played by the redoubtable Anthony Herrera, who was just killed off on *As the World Turns*). Whatever his ultimate role, one can be sure he'll stir things up, and make everyone's problems all the more problematic.

Mike Donovan is troubled, and has been since his return from Vietnam.

Profiles

Wesley Addy
(Cabot Alden)

Fresh from a role in *The Verdict* (with Paul Newman), veteran character actor Wesley Addy portrays the white-haired aristocrat, Cabot Alden, in *Loving*. Early in his career he played in Leslie Howard's production of *Hamlet*, worked in Maurice Evans's repertory company, and trod the boards with Laurence Olivier and Katharine Cornell, as well as with his wife, Celeste Holm. Mr. Addy has put in time in soaps as well, having played Dr. Campbell in *Edge* and Dr. Cooper in *Days of Our Lives*.

Jennifer Ashe
(Lily Slater)

Trained as a ballet dancer, young Jennifer Ashe came to New York from Georgia to study at the American Ballet Theater and with the legendary ballerina, Melissa Hayden. Soon she started making commercials and moved into acting, appearing in off-off-Broadway productions and in the ABC Afterschool Special, *Amy and the Angel*.

Pamela Blair
(Rita Mae Bristow)

Pam Blair, who portrays the lusty wife of coach Billy Bristow, is something of a Broadway star, having played the title role in *Sugar*, Val in *A Chorus Line*, Amber in *The Best Little Whorehouse in Texas*, and Jeunefille in *The King of Hearts*. She also played opposite James Earl Jones in *Of Mice and Men*. She's beginning to rack up credits on TV as well, having appeared in the TV movie, *Svengali*, as well as in *Ryan's Hope* and *Search for Tomorrow*.

Bryan Cranston
(Douglas Donovan)

Loving is the first full-time series for Bryan Cranston, the handsome, green-eyed actor who plays Doug Donovan. But he was brought up in Hollywood, his brother Kyle is an actor, and his dad is a producer, so it's not surprising that "This business is in my blood." He didn't come to acting right away, however; before committing himself to it, he and his brother Kyle motorcycled around the United States for over two years.

John Cunningham
(Garth Slater)

Doing daytime TV in New York City has its advantages; John Cunningham can play the embittered dean of students, Garth Slater, on *Loving* and still costar in the off-Broadway hit, *Quartermaine's Terms*, for which he won an Obie Award. A veteran of Broadway, Mr. Cunningham has played major parts in *Cabaret, Zorba, Company, 1776, California Suite*, and others. On the soaps he's been Dr. Wade Collins in *Search* and Dr. Dan Shearer in *Another World*. He lives in Rye, New York, with his wife, Carolyn, and their three kids, Christopher, Catherine, and Laura.

Shannon Eubanks
(Ann Alden Forbes)

Shannon Eubanks, who plays the elegant and patrician Mrs. Forbes, is in reality an accomplished stage combat choreographer and fencing instructor. Her acting background is classical—she's played more than forty heroines in some eighty productions of plays by Shakespeare, Shaw, Strindberg, and Chekhov—and in fact her interest in fencing grew out of her Shakespearean roles. Born in Charleston, S.C., the green-eyed actress has worked in a number of repertory companies and has appeared in several independent films.

Patricia Kalember
(Merrill Vochek)

Patricia Kalember's first major soap role was as a young investigative reporter on *Texas*. Now the lithe, green-eyed actress is an anchorwoman in *Loving*. But for the most part her experience has been in regional theater in Maryland, Utah, and Pennsylvania. Born in upstate New York, Ms. Kalember grew up in Louisville, Kentucky, and eventually earned a B.F.A. degree at Indiana University, where she met her husband-to-be, actor Mark Torres. The couple lives in Brooklyn.

Teri Keane
(Rose Donovan)

Teri Keane's portrayal of the mother of the Donovan clan is not her first foray into daytime drama. The actress won two press popularity polls for her portrayal of Martha on *The Edge of Night* in 1974. She also played the neurotic mother of Brad Vernon on *One Life*, and earlier played Meg Blaine, the other woman on *As the World Turns*. In the heyday of radio drama, Ms. Keane played in two soaps at the same time: the lovable Chi Chi in *Life Can Be Beautiful* and the witchy Hope in *Big Sister*. She has a grown daughter, Sharon, and baby-sits a 270-year-old stone house in upstate New York.

James Kiberd
(Mike Donovan)

Before coming to the part of Mike Donovan, the disturbed Vietnam vet, James Kiberd had performed in the theater, mostly in upstate New York, but was known primarily as a painter. He studied art at the University of Pennsylvania and won recognition from the National Endowment for the Arts and other organizations. To further confuse any biographer, he has been a woodsman and guide in northern Canada, and still occasionally moonlights as a roofing contractor with his brother in Detroit.

Christopher Marcantel
(Curtis Alden)

Since graduating from the American Academy of Dramatic Arts in Manhattan, young Chris Marcantel has landed parts in three off-Broadway shows: *Missing Persons*, *Geranium*, and *Fugue in a Nursery*. In daytime TV, he's played Pete Shea in *Another World* and Tim Werner in *Guiding Light*.

Arrivals and Departures

Peter Brown
(Roger Forbes)

This doesn't happen. Peter Brown was pumping gas in California one day when Jack Warner of Warner Brothers drove up. Peter introduced himself and the next day got a call at the gas station asking him to come in for a reading. He got a contract and played in a string of two dozen feature films. His career has been as much work as luck, however. He toiled for seven years on *Days of Our Lives* as Dr. Greg Peters and on *Young and Restless* as attorney Robert Laurence. In the fall of 1983 he took over the role of Roger Forbes, the charismatic president of Alden University.

Marilyn McIntyre
(Noreen Vochek Donovan)

Growing up in McLean, Virginia, Marilyn McIntyre started college as an economics major. But then she got the lead in a college production of Ibsen, and the theater bug bit her. Marilyn did graduate work in acting at Penn State as well as in England, and was soon launched in regional and off-Broadway productions, including the New York Shakespeare Festival's *Measure for Measure*. On daytime TV, she was Astrid Collins on *One Life*, Sydney Galloway on *Ryan's Hope*, and Dr. Carolyn Hanley on *Search*.

John Shearin
(Roger Forbes)

Although ultimately deemed not right for the part of Roger Forbes (he left the show at the end of summer), John Shearin has impressive credentials in film, theater, and television, having played in the final episode of M*A*S*H, in *Little House on the Prairie*, and in the late lamented soap, *The Doctors*. He was also in *Comedians* on Broadway and in various off-Broadway and regional productions. A Phi Beta Kappa graduate of the College of William and Mary, Shearin served in Vietnam and went on to produce and direct at Harvard's Summer Rep Theatre before committing himself to his "first love," acting.

Lauren-Marie Taylor
(Stacey Donovan)

Lauren-Marie Taylor, who plays a college athlete, is quite athletic herself, having finished the New York City Marathon well up in the pack in 1981 and 1982. She attended Wagner College and New York University for a while, but gave up academics when she landed a part in *Friday the 13th—Part II*. Soon she won a role in John Belushi's film, *Neighbors*, after which she played in numerous off-Broadway productions. In April 1983, she married actor/songwriter John Didrichsen.

One Life To Live

ABC

The Cast

Gerald
Anthony .... *Marco Dane*

Phylicia Ayers-
Allen............. *Courtney Wright*

Shelly Burch........ *Delila Buchanan*

Anthony Call....... *Herb Callison*

Philip Carey....... *Asa Buchanan*

Marilyn Chris....... *Wanda Wolek*

Roderick Cooke
(left
midyear) .... *Tango*

Nicholas Coster
(joined in
summer)......... *Anthony Makana*

Jacquie Courtney
(left in fall) ...... *Pat Ashley*

Cusie Cram
(joined in
summer)......... *Cassie Callison*

Steven Culp (new
in fall) .... *Don Wolek*

Chris
Cunningham ... *Kevin Riley*

Arlene Dahl (guest
appearances).. *Lucinda Schneck*

Brian Davies
(started
midyear) .... *Scott*

Robert Desiderio
(left in
spring)........... *Steve Piermont*

Christine Ebersole
(joined in
December) ..... *Maxie McDermot*

Jeff Fahey.......... *Gary Corelli*

Steve Fletcher ..... *Brad Vernon*

Al Freeman, Jr...... *Capt. Ed Hall*

Robert Gentry (on
in spring, off in
summer)......... *Giles Morgan*

Anthony
George.......... *Will Vernon*

Sally Gracie .... *Ina Hopkins*

Ava Haddad (left
in spring)........ *Cassie Callison*

Grayson Hall....... *Euphemia*

Tim Hart (new in
fall) .... *Simon*

Roger Hill (joined
in summer)...... *Alec Lowndes*

Ellen Holly (rejoins
cast)............ *Carla Scott*

Margaret
Klenck.......... *Edwina Lewis*

Suzanne
Leuffen .... *Shelley Johnson*

Judith Light .... *Karen Wolek*

Dorian
Lopinto .... *Samantha Vernon*

Judith McConnell
(started
midyear) .... *Eva Vasquez*

Regan
McManus........ *Mary Vernon Karr*

Kristen
Meadows .... *Mimi*

Ken Meeker........ *Rafe Garretson*

William Mooney
(joined in
summer)......... *Paul Martin*

Mary Gordon
Murray........... *Becky Buchanan*

Clint Ritchie........ *Clint Buchanan*

Jeremy Slate
(joined in
summer)......... *Chuck Wilson*

Erika Slezak........ *Victoria Buchanan*

Nancy Snyder ..... *Katrina Karr*

Michael
Storm .... *Larry Wolek*

Robin Strasser ..... *Dorian Callison*

Brynn Thayer....... *Jenny Jansen*

Tim Waldrip
(joined in
spring)........... *Danny Wolek*

A. C. Wery
(appeared and
left) .... *Dick Grant*

Robert S.
Woods........... *Bo Buchanan*

Michael Zaslow
(joined in
summer)......... *David Renaldi (Reynolds)*

Kim Zimmer (joined
in spring, left
midyear) .... *Echo Di Savoy*

Creator:	*Agnes Nixon*
Producer:	*Jean Arley (replacing Joseph Stuart)*
Directors:	*David Pressman, Peter Miner, Larry Auerbach, Allen Fristoe*
Head writer:	*Sam Hall*

Background

Since July 15, 1968, the suburban town of Llanview has been a hotbed of emotional conflict, controversial issues, and underhanded scheming. The beautiful but manipulative businesswoman Dorian Lord Callison, her rival Victoria Lord Buchanan, and the whole lusty, Texas-bred Buchanan family headed by wily Asa, are the characters who form the backbone of the continuing storylines of *One Life to Live*. The show has been honored with a number of Emmy Awards: Robert S. Woods won the 1982–83 Emmy for best actor; Robin Strasser won outstanding actress in 1981–82; and Al Freeman, Jr., won the 1978–79 award for best actor in daytime drama. In its early days, the show pioneered the use of serious social issues (including schizophrenia, frigidity, interethnic marriage, drug addiction) in its scripts, but in recent years greed, glamour, and (of course) lust have tended to edge out sociology.

The Story

Larry Wolek is torn apart when his wife Karen finally gives in to her passion for Steve and runs away with him, first to Nantucket, then to Nova Scotia, where Steve owns land.

In his own way, scheming Asa is also torn: he lusts after Delila (as who wouldn't) but wants to make Mimi his wife. All this is complicated by the irresistible attraction that Delila feels for her cousin Bo. Bo's own feelings for her intensify after he saves her life (wild dogs and hypothermia almost do her in during a photo shoot in a ghost town). Then an old letter turns up suggesting that Bo is Asa's son after all, and therefore not a blood relation of Delila's. Asa's delighted but doesn't tell Bo—the news might bring Delila and Bo together, and old Asa wants her for himself.

Mobsters are thick as thieves in Llanview, and one of them, having agreed to testify, is murdered in the hospital. Jenny noticed a nurse in nonregulation shoes leaving the scene of the crime. Jenny is later shocked to see that Katrina ("Kat") is wearing the same kind of shoes. As Kat prepares to flee to Florida, Captain Ed Hall arrives and arrests her. A man calls Jenny and asks her to meet him; he has information about Tango, the mob's kingpin. But when she arrives the man is

Asa has lust in his heart, but who wouldn't if the object is Delila.

All may look peaceful as Kat and Ina picnic, but intrigue is on the menu. Kat is planning to flee to Florida.

dead. Soon Tango (masquerading as an interior decorator) attempts to kill Jenny, who knows too much. His attempts fail, and under hypnosis she remembers more incriminating details.

Marco's love affair with Edwina would never work, she realizes, and so she gives her affections more and more to Gary, Marco's brother. Just as well; Marco's up to his underhanded tricks: he steals somebody's song and sells it to Becky for $3000.

Edwina just can't make up her mind about Marco. If she's smart, she'll say goodbye to the schemer once and for all.

Edwina, a budding novelist, is stunned when Asa offers her $50,000 to take a leave of absence from the paper and finish her novel. What is that man up to? One thing Asa's up to is Delila, whom he soon marries. But Delila's scheming mother Euphemia seems to be very sick, so Asa is persuaded to fly to Florida and sail his boat to Key Largo with Brad. Delila will fly down to meet them later. But when the boat is far out from land it suddenly explodes. Brad struggles to the shore and eventually makes it to a hospital, but it appears that Asa has met a watery death.

Bo accuses Euphemia of having caused the accident, but she denies all. Although Bo makes love with Becky (who's always been

Only Brad knows that Asa's "watery death" was rigged. He should since he was there.

crazy about him), he's still violently attracted to Delila—his father's apparent widow. Finally, Bo and Delila give in to their passion and make love, at which point Asa turns up alive! He was rescued by drug smugglers. Now he suspects his son Bo of being behind the explosion, because of Delila. Asa devises a scheme to catch his son and Delila together: he has the house bugged. Bo, however, finds the microphone.

It seems someone is trying to frame Kat for the murder of the mobster in the hospital. Jenny, who once suspected Kat, realizes that damaging evidence has been planted in Kat's room. Clearly, the girl is being framed by Tango. Soon Tango decides that Jenny is dangerous and must be killed. Disguised as a decorator, he meets Jenny at the cottage and pulls a gun on her. Luckily, Larry is able to sneak into the room and overpower the villain.

Asa can't resist going to his own funeral (only Brad knows he's alive). Although Delila's in love with Bo, she still has feelings for Asa

Delila may be married to his father, but that doesn't keep her from falling in love with Bo.

Asa and Bo have some harsh words. It's understandable, when you realize they're both in love with the same woman.

and has a hard time delivering the eulogy. Afterwards, in fact, she collapses. Asa rushes up, calling her name. The whole congregation, naturally, is stunned. Later, Bo and his father have a terrific fight about Delila, and Asa banishes Bo and keeps Delila captive. Ultimately, she leaves Asa for Bo. In retaliation, Asa tries to ruin his son.

Delila and Bo look smug now, but Asa's out for revenge.

Marco's back with Edwina and his modeling agency, Dream Faces, has become a legitimate operation. Things seem to be going well for Marco until Edwina becomes jealous of his attentions to Samantha and orders him out of her life.

Dorian (voted Woman of the Year, beating out Vicki) goes off to a spa where she meets the Contessa Echo Di Savoy and her companion Giles. Echo soon shows up in Llanview with a special interest in Clint.

In Clint and Vicki's paper, *The Banner*, a libelous article about Asa has appeared, and Asa sues for $25 million. It turns out he himself was responsible for having the article printed, to get Clint and Vicki kicked off the paper. Dorian could then get control and she and Asa could merge their respective newspapers. Brad foils the plan.

At Dorian's party, Echo appears and Clint finds himself strangely drawn to her, as if he's known her before. Echo maneuvers Clint into stopping by her photographic studio to look at proofs. Later she tries seducing him, and manages to get herself hired on *The Banner*. Soon they are both covering the story of a flood in the Poconos and end up staying in a cabin alone together. Clint is determined to stay faithful to Vicki, but Echo isn't making it easy.

Clint and Vicki have their hands full. It seems Asa's plotting to remove them from The Banner's masthead.

Dorian and Asa are planning a little media merger.

Clint is drawn to Echo, but he doesn't know why she seems so familiar. Is he in for a surprise!

Echo's plan is to seduce Clint and ruin his marriage. She seems to be doing a very good job.

A deranged prison escapee named Dick Grant terrorizes them for more than a day. After he's captured, a rainstorm forces Clint and Echo to spend another night in the cabin. Finally they give in to their passionate attraction. Clint dreams about Gizelle, a woman from his past, and he realizes Echo has been purposely reminding him of her. During a later confrontation, Clint demands to know how Gizelle died. Echo breaks down and yells, "You killed her! You killed my mother!" She has been plotting revenge and now works to destroy Clint's marriage. She seems to succeed, and Vicki leaves town, but only to dig up facts about Echo's background. Indeed, the Buchanan clan rallies to help Clint defeat Echo's plots.

Meanwhile, a new face appears in Llanview: David Renaldi, a concert pianist, father of a teenage girl named Cassie. It turns out that Cassie is David and Dorian's daughter. They try to keep the secret from Dorian's husband and everyone else, including Cassie. The sixteen-year-old comes back from Greece noticeably more grown-up than when she'd left: she's fallen in love with a passionate Greek named Nikos.

Becky is pregnant with Bo's child, and Delila learns she can't have children. Though married to Bo now, Delila is afraid that if he learns these two facts he'll leave her.

Echo pulls her ultimate trick to ruin Clint. She threatens suicide by drowning, lures Clint out to the bridge, then makes it appear that Clint pushed her to her "death." It looks real to Dorian, who reports the "murder" to Captain Ed Hall; but Vicki and Clint realize it was staged. Clint also remembers—finally—how Gizelle had died. It was Echo's father, Arthur, not Clint, who had pushed Gizelle off another bridge those many years ago.

Cassie's father has shown up, but Dorian is trying to keep the news under wraps. How long will she be able to keep that little secret?

Echo's convoluted plot to ruin Clint is a flop and it's certainly a good thing. He hadn't killed her mother after all; her father was the real murderer.

While Clint awaits trial for murder, Echo tools off toward Mexico on a motorcycle. She gets into an accident, and as she lies unconscious a hobo takes her knapsack, which just happens to contain a tape recording of Echo's father ordering her to get revenge on Clint. When the tape finds its way into Clint's hands, he hopes to prove that Echo's disappearance is part of a plot against him. Echo, unfortunately, has succumbed to the great soap opera scourge, amnesia. She is brought back to testify about anything she might remember.

A music box jogs her memory. Clint has discovered a false bottom to it, and in it a note from Gizelle, Echo's mother, saying how much she fears that her husband will kill her. Clint's innocence is now conclusively proven, and a contrite Echo and Giles leave Llanview for Phoenix and a new life.

Vicki is finally able to forgive Clint for his night in the cabin with Echo, and the two are reconciled. Matters do not turn out so well for Bo and Delila. Although delighted to learn that Becky's child is his, he is disgusted when he learns that Delila has lied to him about most things, including the paternity of Becky's child. Bo wants out of the marriage, pronto.

David Renaldi (ne Reynolds) is seeing as much of his daughter Cassie as he can, despite Dorian's opposition. Although he hasn't told Cassie that he's her father, David does recommend her for the music internship she covets (and deserves). Cassie begins to search for her real father, not realizing how close at hand he is. When Dorian accidentally finds out, she's desperate to put a stop to Cassie's investigations.

David, meanwhile, had hoped his smuggling days were behind him; but then a political refugee from San Carlos, a woman named Eva Vasquez, shows up at his door, and before long he gets involved in a dangerous scheme to sneak her into Canada. While David's away, treacherous Scott breaks into his apartment, finds a book that Eva left behind, and has the fingerprints checked. As he suspected, they are Eva's. Clearly, David is again an operative and must be dealt with.

Dorian, meanwhile, has been duped into making fiery speeches in support of San Carlos's brutal junta. Both she and Cassie are manipulated into working against Renaldi. Before long, David suspects that Scott is really an agent, and not just a talent agent. David warns Scott not to say anything to Cassie or he'll kill him.

Although Dorian doesn't want to believe that David is an aider of Latin American terrorists, she becomes convinced when she sees Eva coming out of David's place. Eva has returned from Canada in order to get David involved in a scheme to sell a quarter-million dollars' worth of emeralds, supposedly to finance medical supplies for the San Carlos rebels. Matters come to a boil when the dictator of San Carlos is murdered. When David's away, Scott shows up, demanding that Eva give him a share of the emerald money.

Brad is causing some trouble on the domestic front, sabotaging Katrina's Florida job offer in order to prevent her and Mary from leaving town. Jenny splits up with Brad when she learns what he's done. He also manages to mess up a seance at his hotel, the Vernon Inn. Just as the medium is coming out with some genuine stuff about an old Indian curse on the building, Brad hokes things up with some phony background moaning. The society folks are disgusted and leave. Frustrated, he kicks the wall and to his surprise a panel slides open, revealing a brick wall and a Latin inscription. He breaks through and discovers a passageway—but nothing valuable in it.

David grows suspicious of Simon (another San Carlos refugee), who is smitten by Cassie. Realizing that Scott has bugged Eva's room, David manages to foil Scott's attempt to blackmail her. Eventually, Scott's shenanigans get him killed.

Delila, meanwhile, having tried about every ruse in the book to win Bo back, has ended up as an exotic dancer in Tony's Wildlife Club.

When Herb finds out about David's relationship to Cassie (and by extension, Dorian), he is crushed. Dorian at last realizes that she was manipulated into doubting David's integrity. She now believes in him. Asa, it turns out, has a lot of money invested in San Carlos and was a friend of the country's slain strong man. In fact, a posthumous message comes from the dead dictator: "Beware of Cristofori." Much effort will be expended trying to figure out what this means. A new girl in town, Maxie, has some tantalizing information about it; but for now, she'd like to do some tantalizing of her own. Her object: Bo.

Gerald Anthony
(Marco Dane)

Gerald had an eight-day contract in February 1977, to play Marco Dane, and he's still playing the part. In fact, Gerald Anthony was nominated for an Emmy in 1981–82 for best supporting actor. He started out as a rock and roll singer, landed the lead in a West Coast production of *Jesus Christ Superstar*, and performed in a number of stock company productions before coming to daytime TV. He is married to Brynn Thayer, who plays Jenny on *One Life*.

Shelly Burch
(Delila Ralston Buchanan)

"Statuesque" is the adjective that comes to mind for Shelly. She is an accomplished performer, having created the role of Claudia in the Broadway musical, *Nine*. Earlier she had featured roles in the Broadway productions of *Annie* and *Stop the World, I Want to Get Off*. Daughter of Dean Burch, former FCC chairman and chairman of the Republican National Committee, Shelly grew up among the country's political leaders, and in fact sang "The Star-Spangled Banner" at the 1980 Republican National Convention in Detroit. (Maybe she should be starring in *Capitol*.) Shelly came to *One Life* in 1981.

Philip Carey
(Asa Buchanan)

When the Buchanan clan, headed by wily old Asa, came to Llanview in 1979, it inaugurated Philip Carey's first regular TV role. But the World War II Marine veteran had already had an impressive career in films, appearing with John Wayne in *Operation Pacific*, with Gary Cooper in *Springfield Rifle*, with Henry Fonda in *Mr. Roberts*, and with Tyrone Power in *The Long Grey Line*, among others. He has since appeared in a number of prime-time TV shows and in such stage plays as *Cyrano de Bergerac* and Arthur Miller's *All My Sons*.

Al Freeman, Jr.
(Captain Ed Hall)

Before joining *One Life* in the late 1970s, Al Freeman, Jr., was known as a Broadway actor, having played in James Baldwin's *Blues for Mr. Charlie*, *Golden Boy*, *Look to the Lillies*, and other major shows. He also appeared in a number of off-Broadway plays as well as in Joseph Papp's production of *Long Day's Journey Into Night*. Numerous prime-time TV appearances and Hollywood film roles have increased his recognition. His portrayal of Malcolm X in ABC's *Roots: The Next Generations* received particular acclaim. Mr. Freeman lives in Manhattan with his wife, Sevara.

Margaret Klenck
(Edwina Lewis)

A minister's daughter from upstate New York, Margaret Klenck did graduate work at the American Conservatory Theater in San Francisco, studied mime in Paris, and received training in dance at the National Ballet School of Canada. Before coming to television and *One Life* in the late 1970s, she acquired stage experience in summer stock and in off-Broadway productions.

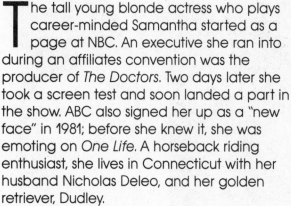

Dorian Lopinto
(Samantha Vernon)

The tall young blonde actress who plays career-minded Samantha started as a page at NBC. An executive she ran into during an affiliates convention was the producer of *The Doctors*. Two days later she took a screen test and soon landed a part in the show. ABC also signed her up as a "new face" in 1981; before she knew it, she was emoting on *One Life*. A horseback riding enthusiast, she lives in Connecticut with her husband Nicholas Deleo, and her golden retriever, Dudley.

Mary Gordon Murray
(Becky Buchanan)

After appearing in Broadway musicals (*I Love My Wife, Grease,* and *The Robber Bridegroom*), Mary Gordon Murray in a sense continues her musical career by playing Becky, a country-western singer, on *One Life.* Born in New Jersey, Mary studied acting at Juilliard and later with Ward Baker at the Herbert Berghof Studio. She joined *One Life* in September 1979.

Clint Ritchie
(Clint Buchanan)

A "North Dakota plowboy," as he calls himself, Clint Ritchie plays a hard-driving Texan, Clint Buchanan, a role he created in 1979. One is not surprised that the rugged actor appeared in the pilot of *Wild Wild West* and in an episode of *Dallas*; but it was a much different role—McMurphy in a stage production of *One Flew Over the Cuckoo's Nest*—which brought him to the attention of 20th-Century-Fox Studios and landed him a contract there. He appeared in several films, including *Patton* and *A Force of One.* Clint owns a horse ranch in northern California.

Erika Slezak
(Victoria Lord Buchanan)

Erika Slezak, who has been on *One Life* for more than a decade, was nominated for a 1983 Emmy as best daytime actress. Daughter of the late actor, Walter Slezak, Erika studied at the Royal Academy of Dramatic Arts in London and for three seasons was a member of the Milwaukee Repertory Company. She and her husband, actor Brian Davies, now live on Long Island, New York, with their two young children, Michael Lawrence (age four) and Amanda Elizabeth (two).

Michael Storm
(Dr. Larry Wolek)

Nominated for an Emmy in 1978, Michael Storm has been playing Larry for more than a dozen years, having taken over the role from his brother Jim Storm in the early days of the show. Raised in California, Michael earned his undergraduate degree in painting. He made his performing debut as a singer on the *Andy Williams Show* and still plays piano and guitar. He and his wife Sally live in Dobbs Ferry, New York, just north of New York City.

Robin Strassser
(Dorian Lord Callison)

Robin Strasser has a knack for playing difficult women. After taking on the role of Rachel on *Another World* for four and a half years, she undertook the role of stubborn Christina Karras Martin on *All My Children*. She then switched to the trouble-making Dorian on *One Life* in the late 1970s. She received the 1981–82 Emmy Award for outstanding actress. But daytime TV has not kept Robin away from Broadway. She starred in *Chapter II* and *The Shadow Box* and coproduced an off-Broadway production of Brecht's *Galileo*. She currently resides in Manhattan with her two sons.

Brynn Thayer
(Jenny Jansen)

Although she had almost no previous acting experience, Brynn Thayer not only managed to land the part of Jenny, but has been able to develop and deepen it over the past four years. The Texas-born actress started out as an elementary school teacher before coming to New York and starting work as a model. She heard about an opening at *One Life* and decided to audition for it. She ended up not only with a part, but with a husband as well, fellow *One Life* actor Gerald Anthony.

Robert S. Woods
(Bo Buchanan)

Robert Woods is a veteran actor *and* a veteran of the Vietnam War, in which he served as a Green Beret for fifteen months. After returning to the States, he majored in broadcasting at California State College and went on to study at the Film Actors Workshop in Los Angeles. Soon he was appearing in a variety of parts in TV, films, and theater. In 1979, he undertook the role of Bo on *One Life* and won the 1982–83 Emmy Award as outstanding daytime actor for his portrayal of the impetuous Texan.

Arrivals and Departures

Jacquie Courtney
(Pat Ashley)

Jacquie Courtney leaves *One Life* after a long and popular run as Pat Ashley. Before joining the show in the mid-seventies, Jacquie played Alice in *Another World* for eleven years. Before that she had roles in *The Secret Storm* and *Our Five Daughters*. In fact, she's spent most of her life on soaps, having started at age twelve on *The Edge of Night*. The blonde, New Jersey-born actress has a daughter, Kristen, with whom she spends as much time as she can.

Judith Light
(Karen Wolek)

Known as one of the great criers on daytime TV, Judith Light leaves *One Life* after a sensational five-year run which netted her two Emmy Awards for outstanding daytime actress. She hopes to make a career in films, and for a start made a TV movie with Tony Geary (of *GH*). The New Jersey-born actress has appeared on and off-Broadway in such plays as *Herzl* and *A Doll's House* (the latter with Liv Ullman). A wine expert and gourmet cook, Judith lived in Manhattan until the call of Hollywood became too strong to resist.

Michael Zaslow
(David Renaldi/Reynolds)

In 1971, Mike Zaslow was appearing in *Fiddler on the Roof* on Broadway when he was tapped for the part of Roger Thorpe on *Guiding Light*. Over the next nine years, Roger Thorpe became one of the most memorable villains on television. Now, three years after Thorpe fell off a cliff, the same face turns up in *One Life to Live*, this time as mysterious concert pianist David Renaldi (or is it Reynolds? Ask Dorian). A native New Yorker in his early forties, Michael worked with his wife Susan on a screenplay, *Allison*; he also writes songs and takes an active (and enthusiastic) part in caring for their adopted daughter, Marika.

Ryan's Hope

ABC

The Cast

Nancy Addison
    Altman............*Jillian Coleridge*
Bernard
    Barrow............*Johnny Ryan*
Dick Briggs..........*Thomas Mendenhall*
Judith Chapman
    (left in
    spring)............*Charlotte Greer Ryan*
Patrick James Clark
    (left in
    spring)............*Dr. Patrick Ryan*
Gloria DeHaven
    (started in
    summer)..........*Bess Shelby*
Jenny Rebecca
    Dweir ....*Ryan Fenelli*
John Gabriel........*Dr. Seneca Beaulac*
Helen
    Gallagher........*Maeve Ryan*
Robin Greer
    (started
    midyear) ....*Sidney Price*
Malcolm Groome
    (resumed role in
    spring)............*Dr. Patrick Ryan*
Ron Hale ....*Dr. Roger Coleridge*
Peter Haskell (left in
    spring)............*Hollis Kirkland*
Marg
    Helgenberger....*Siobhan Novak*
Michael Hennessy
    (started in
    fall)................*Joe Novak*

Earl Hindman ....*Bob Reid*
Christine Jones (left
    in spring) ....*Catsy Kirkland*
Mary Keller (left in
    spring)............*Amanda Kirkland*
Ilene Kristen (left in
    late fall) ....*Delia Coleridge*
Michael Levin.......*Jack Fenelli*
Kelly Maroney (left
    in spring) ....*Kimberly Harris Beaulac*
Malachy
    McCourt..........*Kevin MacGuinness*
Karen Morris-Gowdy
    (left in late
    fall)...............*Dr. Faith Coleridge*
Ariane Munker (on
    show briefly in
    spring)............*Amanda Kirkland*
Will Patton (left in
    spring)............*Ox Knowles*
Geoffrey Pierson
    (started in
    spring)............*Frank Ryan*
Roy Poole (new in
    spring, left in
    summer)..........*Neil MacCurtain*
David Sederholm
    (new in
    summer)..........*Bill Hyde*
Louise Shaffer (left
    in late fall) ....*Rae Woodard*
James Sloyan (left
    in spring) ....*Mitch Bronsky*
Jadrien Steel........*Little John Ryan*
Cali Timmons
    (started
    midyear) ....*Maggie Shelby*
Kathleen Widdoes
    (new in spring,
    left in
    summer)..........*Una MacCurtain*

Creators:	*Claire Labine and Paul Avila Mayer*
Executive Producer:	*Joseph Hardy*
Producer:	*Felicia Minei Behr (replacing Ellen Barrett)*
Directors:	*Lela Swift, Jerry Evans*
Head Writers:	*Claire Labine and Paul Avila Mayer (returned for much of 1983, and left), and Mary Ryan Munistieri. In late fall, head writer is Pat Falken Smith (former head writer at General Hospital and Days of Our Lives).*

Background

Ryan's Hope, which in recent years has won more Emmys for outstanding writing than any other daytime drama, began to stumble in the ratings in 1982 and 1983, after having captured a healthy 32 percent of the daytime audience a couple of years ago. It is one of the youngest soaps, having made its debut on July 7, 1975, and is different from most other soaps in being set in a real place: New York City's Upper West Side.

In fact, reality and authenticity were the qualities that first attracted viewers (and even critics) to *Ryan's Hope*—particularly the psychological reality of the Irish immigrant family headed by the stalwart Johnny and Maeve Ryan. The conflicts between their Old World values and modern urban American life gave a modicum of depth to the usual soap situations (adultery, greed, jealousy, remorse).

Claire Labine and Paul Mayer (the creators and head writers) left the show in 1982, and soon the plot turned to malodorous melodramas of wealth and intrigue. The strong family stories and "tentpole" characters on which the show had been based were moved to the background, and the ratings suffered substantially. In 1983 Labine and Mayer came back to revamp the show. The result was a spring bloodbath during which several storylines (notably the Kirklands') were written out and others written in. Malcolm Groome was brought back after a five-year absence to resume his role as Pat Ryan (replacing Patrick Clark in the role), and the dormant part of Frank Ryan was recast (with Geoffrey Pierson). But still the ratings failed to rebound. Toward the end of the year, Pat Falken Smith (former head writer for *General Hospital*) was brought in as head writer. The results of her efforts will be seen during 1984.

The Story

Flashy Catsy Kirkland's back in town, worried that her disturbed daughter Amanda may remember too much about the past. Catsy's estranged husband, Hollis "Kirk" Kirkland, wants to marry Rae, but can Catsy be convinced to grant a divorce? Matters are made no easier by Rae's illegitimate daughter, Kim, who wants

Kirk to adopt her. "Not possible," he says; but if he can marry Rae, Kim will become legitimate.

Siobhan, posing as a prostitute, has infiltrated the mob and has managed to befriend the mob's psychopathic kingpin, who sets her up in an apartment. In an ensuing police shootout Siobhan is saved, but her rescuer, Mitch Bronsky, is shot to death.

Siobhan is always finding herself in dangerous situations, but then, that's the nature of her business.

Finally, Amanda does remember the past she's blocked out for a decade: she admits to firing the shot that killed Will Brader after he accused Kirk of embezzling money from one of Catsy's companies. These memories have dire implications. If Catsy learned about the embezzlement, she could send Kirk to prison. Panicky Rae asks Pat to give her the tape he made of Amanda's statement. When he refuses, she slams a heavy work cart into his back, knocking him unconscious and accidentally causing an explosion that hurts him badly. The tape, however, is safe in Jack Fenelli's hands.

Seneca confronts Rae with evidence that she was responsible for Pat's near-fatal accident. In order to buy his silence, she agrees to help Seneca gain custody of his and Kim's baby. To this end, Rae pays a film producer she knows $200,000 to give Kim a part in a film being shot in Australia. Kim is elated at this career break and willingly leaves the child with Seneca.

Meanwhile, Catsy has found out about Kirk's embezzlement and thus has total power over him. She decides to keep him and go off to Switzerland. Rae is powerless to do anything about it.

Beautiful Leigh "Marshall" seduces Jack; later she turns out to be Leigh Kirkland, trying to get information about her father. Leigh and Jack begin to fall for each other, but Jack is still haunted by memories

Leigh "Marshall" or Leigh Kirkland? It doesn't really matter to Jack!

of Mary. He will have to go slow in a new relationship.

Frank has returned to the family fold and to everyone's (except Delia's) delight announces he is running for Congress. Alas, Rae vows to combat his campaign with all the power her newspapers and radio stations can muster. Meanwhile, romantic triangles start to jingle: Frank is drawn to his old love, Jill, but devious Delia wants him

Frank hopes to be the new congressman, but he won't be if Rae has her way.

Devious Delia causes trouble again, and Roger takes her to task.

Faith is mad about Pat, but his attention seems to be drawn elsewhere these days.

Amanda's apparent recovery attracts Pat, but appearances can deceive. She's as unstable as ever.

Charlotte Greer Ryan appears on the scene, and brings intrigue with her.

back. And Faith loves Pat, but he's infatuated with the apparently recovered Amanda. Suddenly, a dazzling new woman appears on the scene calling herself Charlotte Greer Ryan. She announces that she and Frank were married and divorced in St. Louis, and that Frank had stolen her money to finance his political ambitions! Frank swears he's never seen the lady before.

When the scandalous publicity gets too hot and Frank's backers waver, it becomes necessary to find a new candidate. Encouraged by Frank, Jill Coleridge decides to run in his place. Determined to learn the truth, Frank abducts Charlotte and interrogates her at his beach house, to little avail. When he lets her go, she skips town.

When Frank's political backing begins to waver, he encourages Jill to run in his place.

Amanda is still unstable, and when she suspects Pat of loving Jill she attempts suicide. Pat and Seneca save her life in the emergency room. Amanda recovers and eventually leaves for San Francisco.

Leigh and Jack Fenelli are in love but both fear marriage. Then Leigh (pressuring her father) buys a TV station and wants Jack to be the news anchor. Proud Jack spurns the offer, but ultimately accepts.

The mystery of Charlotte Greer unfolds. Rae Woodard confesses to Frank that she hired Charlotte to sabotage his campaign. But it's gone beyond that now; something evil has been unleashed. The truth is that Charlotte's father, Neil MacSweeney (known in the old gun-running days in Ireland as Neil MacCurtain), has a life-long grudge against Maeve Ryan, who he feels was responsible for the death of Neil's first wife, his father and his brothers. The plan is to lure Frank and Pat back to Ireland and kill them. Neil's plans change, however, after Rae Woodard interferes and he stabs her, wounding her critically. (She later recovers.) He will now kill Frank Ryan here in New York City and be done with it.

*Will Leigh and Jack's
fear of commitment
stand in the way of
their happiness?*

*Maeve and Johnny's family is
threatened by Neil McSweeney,
a man bent on revenge.*

The confrontation takes place at a deserted waterfront dock. Maeve unexpectedly shows up, Neil tries to shoot her, Frank wrestles with the gun and is critically wounded. He's rushed to the hospital where his life is barely saved. Old Neil dies of a heart attack.

Jill loses the election but is more concerned about Frank. She's followed to the hospital by a woman named Maggie, who claims to be her half-sister. Soon Maggie cons Jill into letting her move into Jill's home. Maggie's motives are larcenous, and she calls her slatternly mother Bess to tell her they're on to something big!

When Maggie stakes a claim to be Jill's half-sister, she and her mother know they've got a good thing going.

Joe had fled from the mob months ago, and Siobhan hasn't heard from him. Besides worrying about Joe, she's tormented by her attraction to Bill Hyde, an attraction that is mutual. At first she tries to resist him but before long they make love.

Roger, meanwhile, has forced Maggie into telling him the truth about her past: that she's really Jill's half-sister but her mother is not the rich, refined lady Maggie has claimed; quite the opposite, in fact. Roger decides to play along with her for the time being.

Finally, a letter arrives from Joe, but the message devastates Siobhan: Joe won't be coming back. She runs to Bill with the news and he comforts her by making love to her and then convinces her to move in with him. But even as they speak, Joe, in another city, is being ordered against his will to return to New York, mob or no mob and Ryans or no Ryans!

On protection duty for a congressman, Siobhan and Bill get to trade their badges for some fancy clothes and go to a night club. There Siobhan is stunned to see Joe Novak. Later, she confronts him and he admits he is married to Jacqueline. Siobhan wants to storm out but Joe stops her, explaining the painful truth: that he had to marry Jacqueline in order to buy his way out of the mob life. In fact, the mob kingpin put it to him that Joe would be killed if he refused. Even worse, Siobhan herself would have been murdered. Devastated by these revelations, she returns to Bill and admits that she's just seen her husband.

Siobhan finds she can't stay away from Joe and arranges to meet him at Tom's old apartment. There they make love and realize again the impossibility of their predicament.

Bess, meanwhile, has shown up in Ryan's Bar in New York and annoys Maeve by flirting with Johnny. Bess is moved when she sees her long-lost daughter, Jill, but does not admit to her who she is. When Maeve and Johnny plan a wedding reception for Jill and Frank, Bess offers to waitress. Unfortunately, she gets a bit tipsy, trips, and falls into the cake! The ceremony nevertheless takes place, and then Maeve and Johnny move everyone to tears by spontaneously renewing their own vows. Alas, Bess has left her apron on the stove and nearly burns the place down. Maggie wants her mother to get out of town, instead of continuing to humiliate her. Bess, though hurt, pipes up that she has every right to be with her two daughters, even though one of them, Jill, doesn't yet know her identity.

Angry at Leigh, Rae Woodard decides she'll break up Leigh's relationship with Jack Fenelli. To that end, she arranges for Jack to be offered a network news job. When asked if she'd recommend him, Leigh's possessiveness takes over and she says that Jack may have a drinking problem. When Rae learns this, she triumphantly tells Jack what Leigh had said. Although Leigh is contrite, Jack is furious that she would say such a thing. Their wedding is called off.

Frank has a favor to ask of Rae. Could she arrange for his ex-wife, Dee, to get a nice splashy out-of-town job so that she'll go off and drop her custody fight for Little John? Rae agrees, and soon Dee gets an offer to manage a club in San Diego. She's delighted, and decides that Jill and Frank will make a wonderful home for Little John. Besides, Dee can still visit on holidays.

Jack would like to patch things up with Leigh, but it's not easy; and his fine-looking lady producer, Sydney, has let him know that she's available. But he resists. Rae makes use of Sydney, however, offering to double her salary and budget if she can get Jack to accept the network job offer. She does her best. Jack, meanwhile, assures Leigh that his relationship with Syd is platonic.

The year ends with Siobhan and Joe still trying to get back together, even though the mob doesn't want them to. And it soon begins to look as though—together or not—somebody is out to kill them!

Profiles

Nancy Addison Altman
(Jillian Coleridge)

An original cast member of *Ryan's Hope*, Nancy Addison Altman is a two-time Emmy nominee (1975–76 and 1977–78). Now in her thirties, she has studied acting with Stella Adler and Sandy Meisner and made her theatrical debut in *The Impossible Years*, with Tom Ewell. Several off-Broadway productions later, she undertook the role of Kim Vestid on *The Guiding Light*, which in turn led to *RH*.

Bernard Barrow
(Johnny Ryan)

As owner of Ryan's Bar and patriarch of the clan, Johnny Ryan represents the old-fashioned values of hard work and devotion to family. The man who plays him, Bernard Barrow, has been an impressively hard worker himself. His long list of credits includes a three-year stint on *The Secret Storm* and a number of other TV and movie roles (including a featured part in *Serpico*). He has also managed to acquire a Ph.D. in theater history from Yale and taught at Brooklyn College from 1955 until his retirement from academe in 1983.

John Gabriel
(Dr. Seneca Beaulac)

John Gabriel stepped out of his Air Force uniform into a contract with 20th-Century-Fox. His first part was a role in Robert Mitchum's *The Hunters* (1958). Since then he's worked at perfecting his craft, as both actor and singer, and has played featured roles in the Broadway production of *Applause* and *The Happy Time*. He's also done a lot of television, including appearances on *The Mary Tyler Moore Show* and *Hart to Hart*. An original cast member of *Ryan's Hope*, Gabriel was nominated for an Emmy in 1979–80 as best daytime actor for his portrayal of the gravely handsome Seneca Beaulac. Now in his mid-forties, Gabriel is a man who just doesn't stop. He has been doing TV commercials, creating and hosting the drop-in TV show, *Soap Spot*, and cutting records. He lives in Manhattan with his wife, Sandy (who plays Edna Thornton on *AMC*), and his children, Melissa and Andrea.

Helen Gallagher
(Maeve Ryan)

Viewers accustomed to thinking of Helen Gallagher as the old-fashioned Maeve should read the rave notices of her performance in the title role of an off-Broadway musical, *Tallulah*, based on the life of Tallulah Bankhead. In fact, Miss Gallagher has been kicking up her heels regularly since 1945, when she joined the Billy Rose production of *The Seven Lively Arts*. From there it was a hop, skip and jump to Broadway's *High Button Shoes*. She's won Tony Awards for her performances in *Pal Joey* and *No, No, Nanette*, and in 1980–81 was nominated for an Emmy Award for her portrayal of Maeve on *Ryan's Hope*, a part she originated when the show first went on the air in 1975.

Ron Hale
(Roger Coleridge)

Don't hiss. Ron Hale is not at all like the conniving Roger Coleridge. Now in his upper thirties, the Michigan-born Hale toyed with the idea of becoming a pro boxer before he came to New York City to try acting. Once there, he studied two years at the Academy of Dramatic Arts, landed roles in *All the President's Men* and other films, played Abelard in the Broadway production of *Heloise*, and did a stint on the TV serial, *Love Is a Many-Splendored Thing*. An original cast member of *Ryan's Hope*, he lives with his wife, Dood, and three children in upstate New York.

Marg Helgenberger
(Siobhan Ryan Novak)

While still a theater student at Northwestern University in Chicago, the stunning red-haired actress played the role of Kate in a university production of *The Taming of the Shrew*. Wouldn't you know, a casting director from ABC TV was in the audience looking for new talent. Marg finished her studies and came to New York, where since 1982 she's been playing the part of Siobhan on *RH*. Still in her early twenties, Marg has been getting a lot of on-the-job training and making a strong mark for herself on the show.

Earl Hindman
(Bob Reid)

Brought up in Tucson, Arizona, tall, lantern-jawed Earl Hindman got into acting while at the University of Arizona. Between semesters, he landed his first professional Shakespearean role at the Old Globe Theatre in San Diego; he liked it so much that he quit school and plunged into the world of repertory theater, eventually ending up in New York in several off-Broadway and Broadway parts. He appeared in the Richard Pryor movie, *Greased Lightning*, as well as in Warren Beatty's *The Parallax View* and other films. After brief daytime roles on *The Doctors* and *Search*, Earl came to *Ryan's Hope* as an original cast member, playing Bob Reid, Frank Ryan's best friend and occasional campaign manager. He lives in Connecticut with his wife, the former Mollie McGreevy.

Michael Levin
(Jack Fenelli)

Jack Fenelli is a central figure in the Ryan/Fenelli/Coleridge triad of storylines, and Michael Levin has played him since the show's debut. Although this is his first role on daytime TV, he's been honored with three consecutive Emmy nominations for best daytime actor. Mike Levin started out as a stage actor, beginning at the Guthrie Theatre in Minneapolis in 1963. He went on to a major role in the Broadway production of *The Royal Hunt of the Sun*, as well as Shakespearean roles in Stratford, Connecticut. He lives in Westchester, New York, with his wife and two children.

Arrivals and Departures

Gloria DeHaven
(Bess Shelby)

Since her screen debut at the age of nine in Charlie Chaplin's classic, *Modern Times*, Gloria DeHaven has appeared in over forty movies, most of them musicals. She is especially fond of *Two Girls and a Sailor*, because it catapulted her and her two costars, June Allyson and Van Johnson, to fame. Other actors she has starred with include Frank Sinatra, Roz Russell, Tony Curtis, even Nancy Reagan (they played sisters in *The Doctors and the Girl*). Now in her late fifties, Miss DeHaven has appeared frequently on TV, including a year-and-a-half stint playing Sara Fuller on *As the World Turns*.

Malcolm Groome
(Dr. Patrick Ryan)

An original cast member, Malcolm Groome left the role of Pat Ryan after three years to follow the lure of Hollywood. He landed roles in several prime-time series, including *Eight Is Enough* and *Hill Street Blues*, as well as in an ABC Afterschool Special, "A Matter of Time." Early this year, he returned to *RH* to resume the part of Pat Ryan, which he originated.

Ilene Kristen
(Delia Coleridge)

Ilene Kristen played the role of the blonde schemer, Delia, then left the show, only to return in 1982. In the fall of 1983, her part was (at least for now) written out. A native New Yorker, Ilene graduated from the Professional Children's School and made her Broadway debut as a dancer in *Henry Sweet Henry*. She later originated the role of Patty Simcox in the Broadway hit, *Grease*. She's also directed several plays (*Street Venus* and *Accumulated Baggage*) and produced the award-winning short, *The Aftermath*. During her three-year "vacation" from *Ryan's Hope*, she sought her fortune in Hollywood, playing Peter Falk's sister-in-law in the Cassavetes film, *Knives*. Ilene is also a rock and roll singer and has recorded numerous songs, including "Giveaway," which she wrote herself.

Karen Morris-Gowdy
(Dr. Faith Coleridge)

Having grown up on a cattle ranch in Wyoming, Karen decided to see more of the U.S. A bit of luck came her way in 1974, when she was crowned America's Junior Miss, an honor which not only landed her a scholarship at the University of Wyoming but sent her traveling all around the country as well. She ended up in New York, studied theater at N.Y.U., and four years ago landed the role of Faith on *RH*. She left the show at the end of 1983. She is married to Curt Gowdy, Jr., a producer for ABC Sports.

David Sederholm
(Bill Hyde)

The guy is bright, having whizzed through Harvard in three years, majoring in philosophy and emerging magna cum laude. He's also proving himself to be something of a heartthrob on daytime TV since taking on the role of macho Bill Hyde in mid-1983. The Philadelphia-born actor did a two-year stint in the Peace Corps in the South Pacific starting in 1973, then spent another two years working for Exxon before he began getting small acting parts on TV. Bill Hyde is his first major role.

Louise Shaffer
(Rae Woodard)

The tall, blonde, Connecticut-born actress was honored with an Emmy Award in 1982–83 as best supporting actress in daytime drama for her role as the manipulative Rae Woodard, a part Louise played for the past six years before leaving the show at the end of 1983. She has also played in various other soaps, including *Search for Tomorrow, Edge of Night, Where the Heart Is,* and Norman Lear's adult soap opera, *All That Glitters.* She lives in Manhattan with her husband, producer-writer Roger Crews.

As The World Turns

CBS

The Cast

Hillary Bailey (started summer)............. *Margo Montgomery Hughes*
Mary Lynn Blanks....... *Annie Ward*
Judith Blazer............ *Ariel Dixon*
Brian Bloom (started April 1983)............ *Dustin Donovan*
Patricia Bruder......... *Ellen Stewart*
Scott Bryce .... *Craig Montgomery*
Larry Bryggman........ *Dr. John Dixon*
Margaret Colin (left midyear) .... *Margo Montgomery Hughes*
Matthew Cowles (in spring only).......... *Lonnie*
Vicky Dawson (left in May 1983)............ *Dee Stewart*
Justin Deas .... *Tom Hughes*
David Forsyth (left in fall) .... *Burke Donovan*
Henderson Forsythe.............. *Dr. David Stewart*
Eileen Fulton (left midyear) .... *Lisa McColl*
Don Hastings .... *Dr. Bob Hughes*
Eddie Earl Hatch........ *Tucker Foster*
Kathryn Hays............ *Kim Andropolous*
Anthony Herrera (left in late fall) .... *James Stenbeck*
Avra Holt (in spring only).................. *Bobbi Maxwell*
Robert Horton .... *Whit McColl*
Chris LeBlanc (started May 1983)............ *Kirk McColl*
Robert Lipton .... *Dr. Jeff Ward*
Lisa Loring .... *Cricket Montgomery*
Juanita Mahone (started February 1983)................. *Samantha Jones*
W. T. Martin............. *Stan Holden*
Kathy McNeil .... *Karen Haines Stenbeck*

Lee Meredith (started in June 1983)......... *Charmane L'Amour*
Hugo Napier............ *Gunnar Stenbeck*
Jacques Perreault...... *Frank Andropolous*
Danny Pintauro........ *Paul Stenbeck*
Elaine Princi .... *Miranda Hughes*
Mary Linda Rapelye.............. *Maggie Crawford*
Frank Runyeon.......... *Steve Andropolous*
Leon Russom (new in late fall) .... *Dr. Zachary Stone*
Meg Ryan............... *Betsy Stewart Montgomery*
Norman Snow (new in late fall) .... *Richard Fairchild III*
Anne Sward............ *Lyla Montgomery*
Frank Telfer............. *Brian McColl*
Marisa Tomei (new in late fall) .... *Marcy Thompson*
Kim Ulrich (started March 1983)......... *Diana McColl*
Terri Vandenbosch (started May 1983)................. *Frannie Hughes*
Betsy von Furstenberg (started midyear) .... *Lisa McColl*
Colleen Zenk .... *Barbara Stenbeck*

Executive Producer: *Mary-Ellis Bunim*
Producers: *Michael Laibson, Brenda Greenberg*
Associate Producer: *Bonnie Bogard (replaces Susan D. Lee)*
Directors: *Paul Lammers, Richard Dunlap, Peter Brinckerhoff, Maria Wagner*
Writers: *Caroline Franz and John Saffron, with Tom King, Chuck and Patti DiZenzo, Lynda Myles, Millee Taggart*

Background

Jeff and Annie's quadruplets, James Stenbeck's blackmailing schemes, Tom and Margo's impromptu come-as-you-are wedding, a murder trial that ends with the "victim" walking into the courtroom—these are some of the more startling elements in 1983's storylines on the venerable *As the World Turns*. Actress Helen Wagner, who originated the role of Nancy Hughes when *ATWT* premiered in 1956, made a special appearance at the wedding of Tom and Margo—an outdoor affair set in Oakdale's Sunset Park (in reality, a bloom-filled arboretum on Long Island, New York).

Created originally as a radio drama by the legendary Irna Philips, *ATWT* made the switch to television twenty-eight years ago, becoming the first half-hour TV soap opera. In 1975, the show expanded to an hour, allowing greater scope for the tribulations of the Hughes, McColl, and Stewart families. As with all serials, the story is filled with who's: Barbara Stenbeck, for instance, who is married to adventurer Gunnar Stenbeck, who helped her gain custody of her son from her ex-husband, James Stenbeck, who is now married to Karen, who blackmailed him into marriage using information she got from Dr. John Dixon, who's the father of Margo and Cricket Montgomery. In fact, it would take a *Who's Who* to straighten it all out.

On May 20, 1983, the seven thousandth episode was broadcast to an estimated audience of twelve million. Despite occasional on-location diversions in Spain, Jamaica and Greece, the stories remain rooted, as always, in the mythical Midwestern town of Oakdale.

The Story

January starts with a bang, as that desperate schemer James Stenbeck accidentally (but nonfatally) shoots himself while trying to do in his estranged wife Barbara and the man she loves, James's cousin and nemesis, Gunnar.

Betsy Stewart, though still sweet on trucker Steve Andropolous, marries ambitious Craig Montgomery, who turns out to have a problem with impotence and infertility. His sister, rookie cop Margo, has

Gunnar and James just do not get along. Of course, the fact that Gunnar is in love with James's estranged wife may have something to do with it.

Betsy makes a big mistake when she marries Craig instead of Steve.

It's a happy day for Gunnar and Barbara when they are finally free to marry.

no infertility problems and in fact is pregnant. She won't tell her fiance, attorney Tom Hughes, about it though, since they're at the point of breaking up. The bone of contention between them is an upcoming trial, in which Dee Stewart is accused of murdering Margo's father, Dr. John Dixon. Tom's insistence on defending Dee appalls and outrages Margo.

As it happens, several people have motives to kill Dixon, among them the unscrupulous James Stenbeck, who is really not a Stenbeck at all and therefore ineligible for the Stenbeck fortune. It seems Dixon had known this and was blackmailing James.

When her divorce from Stenbeck becomes final, Barbara promptly accepts an engagement ring from her true love, Gunnar. Meanwhile, Tom Hughes has been grilling his own true love, Margo, on the witness stand, after which trauma she drags herself to a hospital and miscarries. The trial ends abruptly when the "murdered" man, John Dixon, shows up in the courtroom. He claims he had to fake his death or James would have killed him for real. As punishment for this hoax, John is ordered by the judge to practice medicine three days a week at the penitentiary for a period of two years.

That's the least of John's problems. Dee, the woman he loves, has agreed to marry his enemy, James. Those marriage plans will be thwarted through the chicanery of Karen Haines, who wants to marry him herself—for money. She's given up on love, after having lost out with Dr. Jeff Ward. And well she might give up, since Jeff and his wife Annie have just produced quadruplets!

Blackmailed into marrying Karen, James does not even kiss his bride at the wedding. Things work out better for Tom and Margo,

Everyone knows where Jeff and Annie Ward will be spending their nights for the next few years. They're holding their newborn quadruplets!

who get back together and stage a madcap, spontaneous, open-air wedding the first week in June.

Meanwhile, Steve Andropolous's truck has been blown up, and Craig Montgomery—who was behind the deed—spreads the rumor that Steve did it himself, for the insurance money. The volatile combination of jealousy and infertility will later drive Craig to even worse persecutions of Steve, especially when Craig's wife Betsy becomes pregnant. During a costume party in late June, Craig steals a collection of precious coins, transfers Steve's fingerprints onto the box,

Tom and Margo's wedding is a high-spirited, come-as-you-are affair.

and hides the loot in Steve's room. Police come to arrest Steve, but he makes a desperate escape, during which he's shot in the leg. Hidden and helped by Betsy, he refuses to give himself up until he can prove his innocence.

Life is, if possible, even grimmer for James, who has lost custody of his son Paul to Barbara (now married to Gunnar). Worse, James's sister Ariel intercepts a letter to him from a horse-trainer named Burke Donovan. Burke hates Gunnar as much as James does. He thinks Gunnar caused his wife Nicole's death and fathered the boy known as Dusty Donovan. Ariel immediately grasps that this means Gunnar (through Dusty) is the one in line for the Stenbeck fortune. Ariel swears Burke to secrecy, but conniving Karen soon finds out. James, meanwhile, still thinks that everything hinges on his boy, Paul, and he tries various stratagems, including kidnapping, to get the boy back. Fortunately, his nefarious plots do not succeed.

James and Burke decide to try to make Gunnar believe that he drove Nicole to suicide. They deliver to him a phony newspaper article that says she killed herself because she was abandoned by a former lover who'd made her pregnant. Gunnar is stunned, and shortly afterwards runs into a Nicole look-alike. Gunnar eventually confesses to Barbara about his past with Nicole. He thinks he's hallucinating and begins to fear for his sanity. That's just what Stenbeck wants. But the scheme soon backfires.

About then Miss Charmane L'Amour shows up, claiming that she is legally married to Whit McColl. That's unfortunate since he's married to Lisa.

Nothing seems to go right for James. First he loses Barbara to Gunnar, and now he's lost custody of his son, Paul, to the two of them.

Is Whit going to be proved a bigamist? He will be if Miss Charmane L'Amour has her way, and where will that leave Lisa?

Burke turns out to have Wilhelm's disease and could die very soon. A justice of the peace is called so that Burke and Ariel can be married in the hospital room. His difficult son Dustin shows up and objects—he says Ariel hates him—so the wedding is delayed.

Betsy, meanwhile, is still hiding the wounded Steve. When he's almost caught, he runs off and joins a traveling circus. Later he hides in the basement of an exercise salon. Soon Bobbi's vicious boyfriend Lonnie traps Betsy and Steve at knifepoint and ties them up. He wants the $25,000 reward offered by the police for Steve's capture. Steve's friend Tucker comes to the rescue in the nick of time.

Though Betsy is in some danger of losing her baby, she gets herself and Steve onto a boat to Bermuda, using the names Mr. and Mrs. Daniel Bishop. They pledge their love to each other, but finally Steve decides to return to Oakdale and turn himself in.

Burke Donovan, in the hospital, takes a turn for the worse and it's soon evident that he's dying. Karen, who has already fallen in love with John, tells Burke how fond she is of him and of his boy Dustin.

Craig's bad investments have wiped him and Betsy out of the stock market. When Craig learns that the crooked coin dealer, Vermeil, is on the same cruise ship as Betsy, he boards the boat in Nassau, narrowly misses running into Steve, and sells one of the stolen coins to Vermeil for $10,000.

When Gunnar and Barbara show up after Burke's funeral, a distraught Ariel cries that Gunnar is responsible for Burke's death, and that Burke was once married to Nicole! Gunnar realizes that if this is true, Dustin might really be his and Nicole's child—not Burke's at all. This could mean Gunnar is in line for the Stenbeck fortune.

Karen is now determined to divorce the awful James Stenbeck and hopes one day to marry John. Young Dustin agrees that that would be okay with him. After John threatens to expose James Stenbeck as the crook, Jim Aldrin, Stenbeck finally agrees to give Karen a divorce.

Arriving home, Betsy tells Craig that she's leaving him. (This is after Craig has already proposed to and been rejected by Diana McColl.)

Later, when she's in the boat house with Steve, Betsy goes into labor. Even though he's still a fugitive, Steve gets her to the hospital and waits in the shadows until the premature but healthy baby is delivered. Unfortunately Steve is arrested before he can slip away. The baby is named Danielle.

Meanwhile Karen and John have taken Dustin and flown down to the island of Hispanique where she can get a quicky divorce from James and a quicky marriage to John. Although James finds a legal pretext to stop the divorce, he and Ariel arrive in Hispanique a few minutes too late. Karen is divorced and remarried!

James comes up with another plan to get the Stenbeck fortune. Ariel will win Gunnar away from Barbara, get hold of the money, then split it with James. Ariel gives it a try, but it doesn't work. Gunnar and John hire a small private plane to take them home from the island. As the plane gains altitude, Gunnar and the other passengers have trouble breathing. It turns out James is up front flying the plane and he's the only one with an oxygen mask. Everybody passes out except James, but then Gunnar revives and struggles with Stenbeck. Finally the villain falls out the open hatch to his richly deserved death!

Gunnar manages to crash-land in the Everglades, and after slogging through the swamps just ahead of a threatening hurricane, everyone is rescued. Dusty learns that he's Gunnar's son and realizes that John and Karen are after the Stenbeck fortune. But when the Stenbeck fortune finally does come to Gunnar, he and his good wife decide to donate it all to an orphanage.

As the year winds up, Frank Andropolous, Steve's cousin, appears; he's a reporter and former cop and helps get the goods on Craig. Steve himself is cleared of all charges.

Craig, meanwhile, has found a way to hold onto Betsy a while longer. After picking up pointers from a stuntman, Craig fakes a fall down a flight of stairs and pretends to be paralyzed. When Betsy agrees to stay with Craig until he recovers, Steve reacts by turning his attention to the beautiful Diana McColl.

Marcy Thompson, an injured patient of Dr. Bob Hughes's, comes on to Dr. Bob in the hospital—even strips before him. Naturally, John Dixon happens to observe all this and stores the information away for future use.

Another new character, the mysterious Richard Fairchild III, shows up and soon falls hard for Barbara. He is not, however, quite as wealthy or genteel as he makes out.

Jeff Ward, who has struggled all year with his drug problem, continues to struggle and backslide right to the end of 1983, and in the process very nearly ruins his marriage.

Tom and Margo decide to have a baby. Unfortunately, Margo has volunteered to be a "Muggable Mary" decoy to catch crooks. Tom doesn't love that idea, especially now when Margo is trying to get pregnant. But we all know how headstrong that Margo can be.

Profiles

Mary Lynn Blanks
(Dr. Annie Ward)

Her father's job with an airline permitted Mary Lynn Blanks to see the world when she was young—including Russia, Japan, Turkey and India. Later, while at Florida State University, she joined the Pied Piper Players, a traveling children's theater group. The holder of an FAA pilot's license, she's also skilled at skin diving and has had circus training. She joined *ATWT* in July 1982.

Judith Blazer
(Ariel Dixon)

A New Jersey girl, Judith Blazer originated the role of Ariel in January 1982. It was the first TV part for this operatic soprano, a graduate of the Manhattan School of Music. During her career, she has soloed with various orchestras at Carnegie Hall and was in the cast of the off-Broadway show, *The Fantasticks*. She plays the violin, trumpet, and recorder.

Scott Bryce
(Craig Montgomery)

In April 1982, Scott Bryce created the role of the hissably ambitious Craig. It was the first recurring TV role for the son of soap actor Ed Bryce (Bill Bauer on *Guiding Light*). Scott has done regional theater and appeared in the Broadway production of Shaw's *Caesar and Cleopatra*. In his free time, he produces music videos and plays guitar.

Larry Bryggman
(Dr. John Dixon)

A veteran stage actor, Larry Bryggman has been praised for his many off-Broadway roles, including his part in *Waiting for Godot*. He appeared in a number of productions of the Theatre Company of Boston, and toured with Elke Sommer in *Irma la Douce*. The six-foot Californian joined *ATWT* in 1969.

Justin Deas
(Tom Hughes)

Born in Pennsylvania in 1948, Justin Deas studied acting with John Houseman at the Juilliard School in New York. He's done a wide range of Shakespearean roles, including *Hamlet*. He's also acted off-Broadway, notably in the world premiere of *Crimes of the Heart*. For three years he played Bucky Carter on *Ryan's Hope* before joining *ATWT* in December 1980. He devotes much of his spare time to his fourteen-year-old daughter, Yvie.

Don Hastings
(Dr. Bob Hughes)

Don Hastings joined the national company of *Life with Father* in 1941 and has been acting ever since, appearing in the 1944 Broadway production of *I Remember Mama*. In 1956, he joined *The Edge of Night*, and in October 1960 came to *ATWT*. He married a former *ATWT* cast member, Leslie Denniston, and they have a baby daughter, Katherine. He also has two sons by a previous marriage.

Eddie Earl Hatch
(Tucker Foster)

Eddie Hatch has been playing Steve's trucking partner on the show since October 1982. He's also worked as a fashion model and movie stuntman (doubling for Billy Dee Williams and others), and has been in several films, including *Short Eyes*, as well as in the TV movie, *Muggable Mary*.

Kathryn Hays
(Kim Andropolous)

Kathryn Hays's long TV career has led her to two Emmy nominations for roles in *High Chaparral* and *Star Trek*. She has also appeared in films such as *Counterpoint*, with Charlton Heston, and *The Savage Land*, with George C. Scott. Among her many stage appearances, she and *ATWT* costar Don Hastings toured with a musical concert act, *Hastings and Hays on Love*. She joined the cast of *ATWT* in August 1972.

Robert Horton
(Whit McColl)

The bicoastal actor is perhaps best known for his role as Flint McCullough on the *Wagon Train* series, in which he starred for five seasons; but his years on *ATWT* are making the character of Whit McColl equally famous. Robert Horton's prime hobby is flying, and he's logged over a thousand hours at the controls of his own plane.

Lisa Loring
(Cricket Montgomery)

Born in the South Pacific in 1958, Lisa Loring grew up in Los Angeles. At age eight, she played the role of Wednesday on *The Addams Family*. Since then, she's appeared on a number of other TV shows and commercials. In June 1980 she came to New York to originate the role of Cricket on *ATWT*.

Kathy McNeil
(Karen Haines Stenbeck)

Kathy McNeil's first major television challenge was to create the steely-eyed character of Karen Haines. That was in October 1981. Before that Kathy, a Philadelphian, earned a B.F.A. in acting at Ithaca College and went on to do graduate work at the theater school of Circle in the Square, in New York. She has two sisters, one of whom is a doctor.

Hugo Napier
(Gunnar Stenbeck)

Born and educated in England, Hugo Napier moved to New York City in 1972. He took work at an advertising agency, but his grandmother and her brother had both acted in London's Old Vic company, and the call of the stage proved too strong to resist. He worked in several off-Broadway productions, as well as in the films, *Endless Love* and *Rollover*, before creating the role of romantic adventurer Gunnar Stenbeck in February 1982.

Elaine Princi
(Miranda Hughes)

Before joining *ATWT* in October 1981, Elaine Princi played Nora in a public television production of *A Doll's House* and had roles in *Days of Our Lives* and *The Young and the Restless*. An extensive traveler, she has become proficient at gourmet cooking, fencing, skiing, and horseback riding.

Mary Linda Rapelye
(Maggie Crawford)

After graduating from Wellesley College, Mary Linda Rapelye was picked for a U.S. State Department Cultural Exchange Program tour and performed plays throughout Eastern Europe. She began her television career as a newscaster but quickly moved on to acting roles. In the miniseries *Blind Ambition*, she played Senator Baker's wife. After a brief sojourn at *One Life to Live*, she joined *ATWT* in October 1980.

Frank Runyeon
(Steve Andropolous)

The thirty-year-old Ohioan attended Princeton University and performed in their Triangle Club revues. Later he struggled to make it as a stand-up comedian in New York City, taking typing jobs to support himself. The year 1980 was a good one for him: He joined *ATWT* in May (and quit typing), and got married in June. Frank lives in New York City with his wife and two-year-old daughter, Annie.

Meg Ryan
(Betsy Stewart Montgomery)

If you looked quickly, you could have caught Meg Ryan on *Ryan's Hope* before she came to *ATWT* in July 1982. She also played the role of Debbie in George Cukor's film, *Rich and Famous*. Currently, Meg commutes to New York from the house she shares with two roommates on the Connecticut shore—the perfect place for her to do her daily running (two miles a day) and weekend sailing.

Anne Sward
(Lyla Montgomery)

Anne Sward completed her M.F.A. in acting at the University of Miami and soon came up to New York to study under Herbert Berghof. A contralto singer as well as an actress, Anne sails, hikes, raises Arabian horses, and does charity work to save wild animals that have been abused. She joined *ATWT* in September 1980.

Frank Telfer
(Brian McColl)

Before taking over the role of Brian in December 1982, Frank Telfer did a number of plays in Chicago, then migrated to New York to work off-Broadway in *Barefoot in the Park*. He spent five years as Luke Dancy on *The Doctors*, and briefly played Jeff Martin on *All My Children*. Modeling (with the Wilhelmina Agency) has been another source of income for him.

Colleen Zenk
(Barbara Stenbeck)

Colleen Zenk started dancing at three, appeared on TV when she was five, began modeling at nine, and studied ballet in earnest when she was twelve. Colleen majored in acting at college in Washington, D.C., then came to New York, where she did numerous commercials. A short job on *Ryan's Hope* helped her segue to *ATWT* in September 1978. Her outside interests include interior design, and she hopes one day to obtain a decorator's license.

Arrivals and Departures

Hillary Bailey
(Margo Montgomery Hughes)

This bright-eyed brunette jumped into the part of Margo when Margaret Colin decided not to renew her contract. Hillary has worked in TV (she was a regular on *Family Business*) and has appeared in a few forgettable movies. But her strongest suit is the stage, where she's acted in a dozen plays. She graduated not long ago from Sarah Lawrence College, in New York.

Margaret Colin
(Margo Montgomery Hughes)

Outspoken about the constraints and compromises of the soap opera profession, Margaret Colin has given up her "disgustingly good" salary to brave the uncertainties of New York's theater world. While at Hofstra, she auditioned for and landed a part in *The Edge of Night*, and six months later switched to *ATWT*, where she stayed three years. She lives with her black alleycat, Lucius, on Manhattan's Upper West Side.

Vicky Dawson
(Dee Stewart)

Vicky Dawson joined the show in September 1982 and left the following May, partly, perhaps, because her character had just completed a major storyline and would be on the back burner for a while. A part-time journalism student at New York University, Vicky has gotten good at juggling school and career and would often crack the books in her dressing room at *ATWT*. Now she may have more time for studies.

Eileen Fulton
(Lisa McColl)

Eileen Fulton had let it be known that she wished a greater prominence for her character, and a return to Lisa's former bitchiness. The newspaper articles containing such stories did not, reportedly, sit well with CBS. Whatever the backstage machinations, Eileen left the show in June. She is currently pursuing her singing career.

Anthony Herrera
(James Stenbeck)

Anthony Herrera, who created the character of James Stenbeck in February 1980, has had a lot of soap experience, including parts on *The Young and the Restless*, *Search for Tomorrow*, and *The Secret Storm*. A native of Mississippi, Anthony decided against medical school in favor of acting and came up to New York to study with Stella Adler. He was also associated for a time with the Will Geer Outdoor Shakespeare Theater, an experience which he considers the most memorable of his professional life. He left *ATWT* in the fall.

Chris LeBlanc
(Kirk McColl)

Chris LeBlanc joined the cast in May 1983, in his first recurring TV role, that of troubled teenager Kirk McColl. A commercial talent scout spotted the young actor at Tulane University and started him in local commercials. From there he made appearances on PBS, NBC, and in the film *Cat People*. He has six brothers and sisters rooting for him back in New Orleans.

Juanita Mahone
(Samantha Jones)

Juanita Mahone, who has appeared off-Broadway with the Negro Ensemble Company in their productions of *Colored People's Time* and *Home*, creates the role of police rookie Samantha Jones on *ATWT*. It is her first television role.

Lee Meredith
(Charmane L'Amour)

Lee Meredith debuted in the role of Charmane L'Amour on June 20, 1983. The character (and other characteristics) of the curvaceous Las Vegas lounge lizardette will remind many viewers of Lee's well-remembered role as Zero Mostel's secretary in *The Producers*. She has more recently appeared on Broadway in *The Sunshine Boys* and in *Musical Chairs*.

Kim Ulrich
(Diana McColl)

In March 1983, Kim Ulrich inaugurated the role of Diana, the beautiful, spoiled daughter of a publishing magnate. A one-time entrant in the Miss California beauty pageant, Kim has done regional theater and has had some minor roles on television. She lives a bicoastal life and married actor Robert John Ulrich in 1981.

Terri Vandenbosch
(Frannie Hughes)

A theater major at SUNY Albany, Terri Vandenbosch landed roles in college and regional theaters before making her TV debut on *ATWT* in May 1983, as teenager Frannie Hughes. Like her character, she is a skilled gymnast. Her two younger sisters and a younger brother live in Saratoga, New York, where Terri grew up.

Betsy von Furstenberg
(Lisa McColl)

Betsy von Furstenberg, who replaces Eileen Fulton as Lisa, has played that part before, having filled in for Ms. Fulton several years ago. Born in Germany, she is the daughter of Count Franz-Egon von Furstenberg and Countess von Furstenberg. Betsy made her Broadway debut at seventeen, and has been equally successful on television, where she appeared on *Playhouse 90*, *Alfred Hitchcock Presents*, and *Secret Storm*.

Capitol

CBS

The Cast

Julie Adams
(joined in
spring) .... *Paula Denning*
Kimberly Beck-
Hilton (left
midyear)........ *Julie Clegg*
Bill Beyers........... *Wally McCandless*
Victor Brandt (left
midyear)........ *Danny Donato*
Rory Calhoun ...... *Judson Tyler*
Michael Catlin
(new in
spring) .... *Dr. Thomas McCandless*
Jeff Chamberlain
(left in
spring) .... *Lawrence Barrington*
Todd Curtis .... *Jordy Clegg*
David Mason
Daniels........... *Tyler McCandless*
Christopher
Durham .... *Matt McCandless*
Marj Dusay (new in
spring) .... *Myrna Clegg*
Richard Egan....... *Sam Clegg II*
Duncan Gamble
(left early in
year) .... *Frank Burgess*
Jane Daly Gamble
(left in
spring) .... *Kelly Harper*

Leslie Graves....... *Brenda Clegg*
Catherine Hickland
(new in
midyear)........ *Julie Clegg McCandless*
Carolyn Jones (left
early in
year) .... *Myrna Clegg*
Bradley Lockerman
(new in
midyear)........ *Zed Diamond*
James McKrell
(came and
left)............... *Dr. Parker*
Deborah
Mullowney....... *Sloane Denning*
Wolf Muser (left
midyear)........ *Kurt Voightlander*
Ed Nelson........... *Sen. Mark Denning*
Dawn Parrish .... *Ronnie Angelo*
Julie Parrish (joined
in spring) .... *Maggie Brady*
Kimberly Ross (new
in spring) .... *Amy Burke*
Rodney Saulsberry
(left
midyear)........ *Jeff Johnson*
Todd Starks
(temporary
role) .... *Roge Avery*
Constance
Towers............ *Clarissa McCandless*
Nicholas
Walker .... *Sam "Trey" Clegg III*
Tonja Walker .... *Lisbeth Bachman*
Lana Wood (new in
June)............. *Fran Burke*

Creators:	*Stephen and Elinor Karpf*
Executive Producer:	*John Conboy*
Producer:	*Charlotte Savitz (replacing Stockton Briggle)*
Supervising Producer:	*Patricia Wenig*
Associate Producer:	*Steven Kent*
Directors:	*Rick Bennewitz, Arlene Sanford (replacing Richard Bennett and Bob La Hendro)*
Writers:	*Peggy O'Shea, with Craig Carlson, Steve Hayes, Granville Burgess, David Garrett. (Former head writers, John William Corrington and Joyce Corrington, have left.)*

Background

Perhaps with an eye to the nighttime ratings of shows like *Dynasty* and *Dallas*, the folks at CBS launched a new soap on March 29, 1982, centered on the passions and power struggles of yet another upper-crust American enclave: the political wheelers and dealers in Washington, D.C. *Capitol* concerns two powerful political families, the Cleggs (headed by the spiteful matriarch, Myrna Clegg) and the McCandlesses (headed by the benign matriarchal figure, Clarissa McCandless). The enmity between these women goes back generations, when Clarissa married the man Myrna loved, and it promises to poison relations between the families for generations to come. Against this background is the Romeo-and-Juliet story of handsome Tyler McCandless and young Julie Clegg, star-crossed lovers whom Myrna conspires to keep apart. Unfortunately, during 1982 Julie was afflicted with the most common of soap opera maladies, amnesia, and for quite a while absolutely forgot that she was in love with Tyler. Indeed, the dashing young political aspirant had to rush back from a dangerous mission in N'Shoba just in time to prevent her from marrying someone else! Only on soap operas, you say? Put it this way: if suspending our disbelief were an aerobic exercise, most soap fans would look like Victoria Principal.

The Story

Trey wants to marry Kelly if she'll have him, and to tone up her weak education he helps enroll her at Potomac University. He doesn't know she was a prostitute known as Shelley Granger, who was once used by Frank Burgess to make a blackmail tape. But Brenda knows, and she tells Myrna.

Tyler declines Myrna's invitation for a dinner party for Julie at the Clegg home. The reason: he's now certain that Sam Clegg betrayed the N'Shoba mission. Soon Sam is questioned about this by a House committee, and he storms out. He tells his daughter Julie that Tyler has accused him of being a traitor, and he demands that she choose between the two families once and for all. She sticks with Tyler, but works to clear her dad. Sam, however, continues to refuse to answer the committee's questions.

Julie and Tyler are the Romeo and Juliet of daytime television. Talk about family feuds!

Then Burgess breaks into Danny Donato's office to get the blackmail tape. Danny returns, gunfire is exchanged, and Burgess staggers outside the building and dies. Myrna jumps from her car, seizes the tape and drives off unseen. When she finally views the tape, her suspicions are confirmed: Kelly and Shelley are one. Kelly is convinced that she'll never have Trey now, but they have a make-believe honeymoon together at the ski lodge. She is unable to confess to him about her past before Myrna shows him the damning tape. Kelly sadly packs her bags and heads for the bus depot. Trey learns where she's gone and blocks the bus with his limosine. He and Kelly are reunited.

Not for long, however. Trey burns the blackmail tape, but it soon becomes evident that Kelly/Shelley's past cannot be kept secret indefinitely, not with blackmailers like Donato around. Sam convinces Kelly to break off the relationship with Trey by pretending to be a hooker again. Myrna also offers Kelly a bribe to get out of town. Kelly takes the money, figuring she'll need it to help raise her unborn child. She leaves town without telling Trey he's a father-to-be.

The committee's investigation of Sam has been dropped and ultimately he gives his reluctant permission for Tyler to marry his daughter, Julie.

Myrna is determined to destroy Trey's relationship with Kelly, and when she finds out that Kelly was once a prostitute, she has the ammunition she needs.

The wedding is set for May but is postponed when Tyler's brother Wally is in a serious car accident. He needs a kidney transplant, and his brothers all vie to be the donor. Thomas wins. While Wally is recovering, Brenda tries her best to win his love, even though it is obvious he loves (and is loved by) Ronnie.

Meanwhile, codes are broken that reveal the machinations of Eastern Bloc spies in the sabotage of the N'Shoba mission. Danny's gun, it turns out, did not kill Burgess. The Russian-speaking Kurt and his cohorts were behind it all, Larry Barrington among them. Sloane, the beautiful TV reporter, turns Kurt's gun and a page of code over to Tyler; she agrees to have her apartment bugged in order to help catch the spies.

But when the spies finally are caught, the Cleggs use their power to thwart justice by helping Larry escape. Myrna hires a world-famous attorney to represent Larry (who has threatened to spill Clegg secrets, including Kelly's pregnancy, if he doesn't get off). Ultimately, Kurt kills himself, and Larry decides to cooperate with the authorities, naming foreign agents in return for plastic surgery, a new identity, and a small lifetime allowance.

Trey has sufficiently recovered from the loss of Kelly to begin making determined efforts to seduce Sloane; she takes pleasure in informing him that Tyler's been appointed chief counsel in an investigation of why Trey destroyed government evidence (the Burgess files). It looks like the McCandless/Clegg feud is hotter than ever.

The only way for Trey to continue to survive as a congressman is to discredit Tyler. Vicious allegations are planted in the press, and when Myrna adds her own lies about Wally and Matt, Clarissa for

*Trey certainly got over
Kelly in a hurry.
Sloane has caught his
fancy now.*

once forgets her dignity and slaps the woman! Soon Trey is forced
to resign his committee position, and Tyler announces that he is
running against Trey Clegg for Congress.

Wally insists that Tyler and Julie should not put off their wedding
any longer because of him, and they decide they'll get married in
the hospital. But Myrna and Paula have plans to drop a scandalous

*Sam may have been reluctant,
but he gave his permission for
Julie to marry Tyler, and he's
there to give her away.*

Myrna's at it again. She's hatched a plot to drop a bombshell at Tyler and Julie's wedding.

Senator Denning has fallen for Clarissa, and the feeling is mutual.

bombshell at the wedding. The day (July 22) arrives and the wedding ceremony is performed. But immediately afterwards, Paula is rushed past the wedding party on a stretcher. She has attempted suicide, and she left a note to Senator Mark Denning, saying, "I realize now I've lost you to Clarissa." Mark indeed has fallen for Tyler's mother, and she loves him as well; but Paula's act seems more a calculated ploy (hatched with Myrna) than a true expression of despair. In fact her doctor later accuses her of perpetrating a well-planned hoax. She's no more agoraphobic than he is!

Matt McCandless has become romantically entangled with young Amy Burke. Amy's mother, Fran, owner of the Moon Lake Casino, is dead against the relationship. She tells Amy that Matt is trouble.

Fran Burke is worried. Daughter Amy is in love with Matt McCandless, and Fran doesn't like it.

One evening after closing time, Amy and Fran are counting the day's receipts when two armed hoods break in with robbery and rape on their minds. Brenda, who happens to be nearby, escapes by diving into the lake and swimming to get help. Jordy, Matt, and Brenda arrive at the casino and battle with the thugs, eventually subduing them. Amy suffers temporary blindness, and soon must face the truth: barring a miracle, she'll be blind within a year. She doesn't want to tell Matt that she is losing her sight. She vows to continue her quest to learn who her father is. The possibilities are three: Senator Denning, the deceased Baxter McCandless, or Sam Clegg.

A reluctant Trey teams up with Myrna to find out who Amy's father is. Myrna is stunned when the man turns out to be her husband, Sam. It is one of the few moments when Jordy has ever seen his mother show real pain. Myrna even talks her hurt over with a less-than-sympathetic Trey. And the next day she talks with Amy's mother, Fran. She asks what Fran would do if she discovered who Amy's father was? Fran answers honestly that she'd try to get as much money from him as possible—in order to save Amy's eyesight. Myrna realizes that Fran must never learn that it was Sam.

Soon Sam sees Fran and realizes he is Amy's father. He swears Jordy to secrecy. More secret goings-on include Mark and Clarissa's attempt to have a rendezvous at the Country Inn; their efforts—indirectly because of Paula—are thwarted.

A death threat arrives in the McCandless mailbox. To whom is it directed? Wally thinks Danny may be after him; Judson worries that Paula Denning's gone off the deep end; Tyler theorizes that some screwball is trying to scare him away from politics.

Thomas is preparing to have his back brace removed to see if he can walk without his crutches. He depends on Beth's love and support. Unfortunately, neither his back nor Beth's nerves are strong enough for the test. After another effort, which also fails, and another failure of nerve on Beth's part, Thomas tells her that maybe they'd better call off their relationship for a while.

When Amy learns that she is going blind, she urges Matt to forget about her, but Matt refuses. He is determined to follow her and her mother Fran to Zurich where there is medical hope for a cure. Myrna is behind this sudden move out of the country; she's afraid that Fran may find out about Sam if she stays around.

Wally, pretty well recovered from his transplant operation, is afraid he'll lose Ronnie to a new sharper named Zed Diamond, who has just blown into town and has bought the TV station for which Sloane works; Ronnie denies being attracted to Zed, but harbors secret fantasies of fabulous wealth and the sorts of things she imagines Zed could buy her.

Sloane and Trey are gradually finding each other, and at the end of a particularly romantic weekend in the late fall they pledge their love and look forward to a brilliant political future together. They would, in fact, make a formidable pair if pitted against the vote-getting charisma of Tyler and Julie. But for now, Trey doesn't want the press to know that he and Sloane are an "item." Sloane wonders why not.

Matt has only eight hundred dollars, not really enough to go globetrotting with after Amy. Without getting Matt's permission, Wally takes the money to a poker game and manages to triple it. Ecstatic, Matt takes the bundle and rushes to the airport to join Amy and Fran.

Sam and Jordy arrive at Moon Lake after Amy and her mother have already left. Looking around, Sam vividly recalls his long-ago affair with Fran. He vows that somehow he is going to get his daughter back! Indeed, he wastes no time. When Amy, Fran, and Myrna arrive in Zurich they find Sam waiting for them. After an initial fudging about his identity, the truth comes out. And even though he pays all of Fran's and Amy's expenses, Fran threatens to go to the press with the story of their long-ago affair. Meanwhile, Matt sticks close to his beloved Amy and will not leave her side. He makes an instructive contrast to Beth, who can't stick with Thomas in his time of trouble. Indeed, Beth finds she is still attracted to Jordy. Ah, the fickleness of some women!

Profiles

Bill Beyers
(Wally McCandless)

An original cast member, Bill Beyers boasts a varied background as a performer. He studied dance and singing and for several months attended acting classes with famed teacher Stella Adler in New York. He soon landed a role in the Broadway production of *The Magic Show* and went on to a leading role in the national company of *Grease*. The young, blue-eyed actor's first major TV success was in the role of Frankie in the limited series, *Joe and Valerie*. Three years later he was signed for the role of Wally on *Capitol*.

Rory Calhoun
(Judson Tyler)

The tall (six-foot-three-inch) silver-haired actor has been seen on *Capitol* since the spring of 1982. Rory Calhoun has played a number of television roles, including the part of General Meade in the eight-hour miniseries, *The Blue and the Grey*; but he is primarily known for the more than seventy motion pictures in which he's appeared. It was Alan Ladd's agent wife, Sue Ladd, who saw Rory's screen potential. She helped him win a major role in *The Red House*, with Edward G. Robinson. Since then he has worked with such stars as Marilyn Monroe, Betty Grable, Jean Simmons, Susan Hayward, and Gene Tierney.

David Mason Daniels
(Tyler McCandless)

A sort of better-looking Chris Reeve (and taller by a head), David Mason Daniels has played the central character of Tyler since the spring of 1982. Born in Morristown, New Jersey, David studied sociology at Principia College, where he met his wife, Cheri. After a brief try at a business career, David began making a number of commercials. From there it was a short step to small roles in TV shows. But the role of Tyler is his first major break. He lives with his wife and young son in the San Fernando Valley.

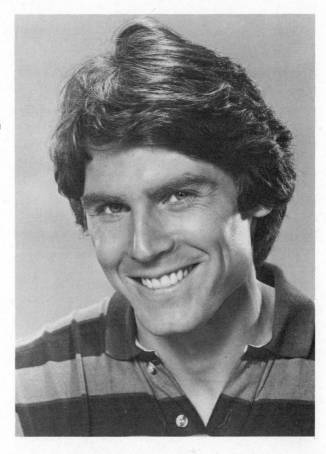

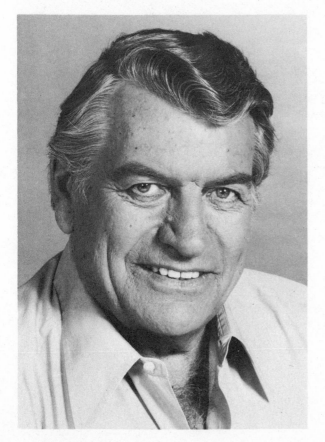

Richard Egan
(Sam Clegg II)

Since the fall of 1982, Dick Egan has played the unscrupulous Sam Clegg on *Capitol*. Now in his fifties, the California-born actor has appeared in numerous films, including *A Summer Place*, *Love Me Tender*, and *Demetrius and the Gladiators*. He's also appeared on stage in Neil Simon's *I Ought to Be in Pictures*, and in *Strike a Match* (costarring Pat O'Brien and Eva Gabor). Married to the former Patricia Hardy, Richard is the father of four daughters and a son.

Deborah Mullowney
(Sloane Denning)

The part of the hard-driving TV reporter, Sloane Denning, is Deborah Mullowney's first television role. Although she has appeared in some community theatre productions, Deborah was making her living primarily as a model before joining the cast of *Capitol*. As a teenager, she signed with the Eileen Ford Agency in New York and later began modeling for Nina Blanchard. She's made a number of national TV commercials and currently lives in Beverly Hills, California.

Ed Nelson
(Sen. Mark Denning)

Born in New Orleans, Ed Nelson threw himself into theater while a student at Tulane University. He appeared in a number of plays with New Orleans's Le Petit Theatre du Vieux Carré before heading to Hollywood for a career in feature films, among them *Elmer Gantry*, *Midway*, *Airport 1975*, and *For the Love of Benji*. He created the role of Dr. Michael Rossi on TV's *Peyton Place* and has guest starred in many TV series. Ed is an original cast member of *Capitol*.

Constance Towers
(Clarissa McCandless)

Constance Towers began her career as a singer and made nightclub appearances at such establishments as Coconut Grove in Los Angeles and the Persian Room in New York City's Plaza Hotel. Soon she found herself in musicals on the Broadway stage and played Julie in the Lincoln Center production of *Showboat*. Among the awards she's received are the New York Critic's Outer Circle Award and the American Academy of Dramatic Arts Achievement Award. On TV, she received an Emmy nomination for her role on the CBS drama special, *Once in Her Life*. She is an original cast member of *Capitol*.

Nicholas Walker
(Sam "Trey" Clegg III)

Born in Bogata, Columbia, Nicholas and his twin brother spent much of their childhood traveling through Europe and South America—wherever their father's international business dealings led the family. Nicholas later earned his Master of Fine Arts degree at the University of California at Irvine. After studying with the redoubtable Brewster Mason of the Royal Shakespeare Company in London and with Uta Hagen in New York, Nicholas made his Broadway debut in Shaw's *Major Barbara*. Since then he has created the role of Brad Huntington on TV's *The Doctors* and has been with *Capitol* since 1982.

Arrivals and Departures

Kimberly Beck-Hilton
(Julie Clegg)

Beautiful Kimberly Beck-Hilton originated the pivotal role of Julie Clegg on *Capitol* and played it until September, when CBS decided to replace her. Kimberly began acting at age two and appeared in *Torpedo Run* as Glenn Ford's little daughter. After high school (in Glendale, California) Kimberly became a cast member of the TV series *Lucas Tanner*, starring David Hartman. Soon Alfred Hitchcock signed her to appear in his film, *Marnie*. Then came a two-year role as a deaf-mute child on TV's *Peyton Place*. Numerous other (more vocal) TV roles followed. Kimberly lives in Malibu with her husband, William Barron Hilton, Jr., a land developer.

Michael Catlin
(Thomas McCandless)

Before joining *Capitol* in June 1983, Michael Catlin played a variety of theater and television roles, and appeared in two feature films, *Celluloid Flash* and *The Captive*. The tall, hazel-eyed actor was born in Ohio and grew up in several Midwestern states, ending up in Chicago during his teens. After two college years spent in the study of economics, philosophy, and political science, Michael realized that he wanted to be an actor, and he majored in theater at the University of Minnesota. Soon he was performing in regional theater productions of *Tom Jones*, *The Threepenny Opera*, *Godspell*, and other shows. He continued his stage career in Los Angeles (appearing in *Kennedy's Children*, among others) and began getting work in TV shows such as *CHiPs* and *Knight Rider*. When not working, Michael plays paddle tennis and body surfs. he's also involved in the End Hunger Network.

Marj Dusay
(Myrna Clegg)

After Carolyn Jones became ill and withdrew from the part of Myrna early in the year, actress Marla Adams took over for a short while, and then Marj Dusay was cast in the role. The Kansas-born actress modeled and made TV commercials before making her stage debut in 1965 in Shaw's *Man and Superman*. In 1966, two struggling young actors, Rob Reiner and Richard Dreyfuss, invited Marj to join The Session, an improvisational comedy group. Numerous TV credits were soon hers, culminating in the enviable role of scheming Myrna.

Jane Daly-Gamble
(Kelly Harper)

Philadelphia-born Jane Daly moved to Florida when she was ten, went to college at the University of Denver, then came east to New York City to study acting. She did a number of commercials in New York before zipping west to Los Angeles to pursue a film career. Her film credits include *North Dallas Forty* and *The Black Marble*. The major role of Kelly Harper was written out of *Capitol* in the spring, but if Jane lost a part she gained a husband. In 1982 she married Duncan Gamble, who played her nemesis Frank Burgess on the show.

Carolyn Jones
(Myrna Clegg)

The elegant, Texas-born actress had a long and illustrious career in films and television before she became an original (and centrally important) cast member of *Capitol*. She played many kinds of roles, from the lonely Greenwich Village existentialist in Paddy Chayefsky's film *Bachelor Party* to the unforgettable Morticia on *The Addams Family*. She died in August, after a long struggle with cancer.

Lana Wood
(Fran Burke)

Although never as famous as her sister Natalie, Lana Wood has had an impressive career in films and television. Her first speaking part came her way at age eight, when she appeared with John Wayne in *The Searchers*. Regular roles in the TV series *The Long Hot Summer* and *Peyton Place* followed some years later, as well as parts in films, including *Speedtrap* and *Diamonds Are Forever*. Besides acting, Lana has been active in developing and producing properties for television. She joined the cast of *Capitol* in June 1983.

Guiding Light
CBS

The Cast

Rose Alaio (left in
    spring)............. *Helena Manzini*
Grant
    Aleksander......... *Philip Spaulding*
Elizabeth Allen
    (temporary
    role) .... *Dr. Gwen Harding*
Charita Bauer .... *Bert Bauer*
Gregory
    Beecroft............ *Tony Reardon*
Christopher
    Bernau.............. *Alan Spaulding*
Lisa Brown............ *Nola Chamberlain*
Ed Bryce (special
    appearances).... *Bill Bauer*
Warren Burton (new
    in spring)........... *Warren Andrews*
Carolyn Ann
    Clark.............. *Lesley Ann Monroe*
Marsha Clark .... *Hillary Bauer*
Richard Clark (left
    early in year) ...... *Bryan Lister*
Jordan Clarke (new
    in spring).......... *Billy Lewis*
Jennifer Cooke (left
    in spring).......... *Morgan Nelson*
Geraldine Court (left
    in spring).......... *Jennifer Evans*
Kathleen Cullen (left
    in spring).......... *Amanda Spaulding*
Ellen Dolan........... *Maureen Bauer*
Judi Evans (new in
    spring).............. *Beth Raines*
Beulah Garrick (left in
    spring).............. *Violet Renfield*
Larry Gates (new in
    midyear) .... *H. B. Lewis*
Janet Grey (left in
    spring).............. *Eve McFarren*
Rebecca Hollen...... *Trish Lewis*

Stephen Joyce
    (started
    midyear) .... *Eli Sims*
Maeve Kinkead ...... *Vanessa Chamberlain*
Harley Kozak (new
    this spring) .... *Annabelle Sims*
Lee Lawson .... *Bea Reardon*
Robert Newman...... *Josh Lewis*
Tom Nielsen.......... *Floyd Parker*
Leslie O'Hara (left in
    spring).............. *Rebecca Cartwright*
Michael O'Leary...... *Rick Bauer*
Thomas O'Rourke (left
    in spring).......... *Dr. Justin Marler*
Denise Pence......... *Katie Parker*
Mark Pinter (left in
    spring).............. *Mark Evans*
Susan Pratt (new in
    spring).............. *Dr. Claire Ramsey*
James Rebhorn (new
    in spring).......... *Bradley Raines*
William Roerick....... *Henry Chamberlain*
Elvera Roussel (left in
    late fall)........... *Hope Spaulding*
John Wesley
    Shipp .... *Dr. Kelly Nelson*
Peter Simon .... *Dr. Ed Bauer*
Tina Sloan (new this
    spring).............. *Lillian Raines*
Don Stewart........... *Michael Bauer*
Krista Tesreau (new in
    spring).............. *Mindy Lewis*
Michael Tylo .... *Quinton Chamberlain*
Jerry ver Dorn .... *Ross Marler*
Michael Woods (new
    in late fall) .... *Dr. John Stevens*
Kim Zimmer (new in
    late fall) .... *Riva Lewis*

Creator:	*Irna Phillips*
Executive Producer:	*Gail Kobe (replacing Allen M. Potter, now at Another World)*
Producers:	*Leslie Kwartin, Robert Calhoun (who replaces Joe Willmore)*
Associate Producer:	*Janet Stampfl*
Directors:	*Harry Eggart, Bruce Barry, John Whitesell*
Writers:	*Pamela Long Hammer and Richard Culliton; with Carolyn DeMoney Culliton, Samuel D. Ratcliff, Trent Jones, John Kuntz, Michelle Poteet Lisanti, Cynthia Saltzman, Addie Walsh (replacing L. Virginia Browne and her writing staff)*

Background

One of the longest-running soaps on the air, *Guiding Light* was first seen in June 1952. But it was *heard* much earlier than that, having been created as a fifteen-minute radio drama by Irna Phillips in 1937. That's nearly half a century of storyline. For close to thirty-four of those years, the head of the close-knit Bauer family has been played by Charita Bauer, a highly professional and much loved actress who has no patience for primadonnas and no inclination to be one. The mythical midwestern town of Springfield is the setting for the joys and tribulations of the Bauer and Reardon families, as well as the Marlers, the Chamberlains and the wealthy Spauldings.

The year 1983 has not been an easy one on the set of *Guiding Light*. When Gail Kobe took over as executive producer, she made sweeping changes resulting in a bloodbath of cancelled storylines and a transfusion of new (and generally young) characters. Confusion and a degree of demoralization struck some of the veteran actors who had managed to escape the axe. By a coincidence that could be viewed as symbolic, Charita Bauer became very ill in late summer and through the fall, first with pneumonia, then with blood clots and diabetes. Everyone hopes that she is back on the show early in 1984. If not, *GL* will be quite a different program.

Whether all the changes will shake the loyalty of longtime *GL* fans is a major question. Answers should come in the next few months as the new storylines take hold.

The Story

Rebecca tries through various means (including pretending that she can't speak) to maintain her hold over Quint, even though she knows he is in love with Nola. Quint hopes that once Rebecca is "well" he can propose to Nola. But Rebecca's continual scheming leads to a car crash which nearly kills Quint. At the hospital, Nola learns that Quint is really Henry Chamberlain's son. Quint is furious that she's found out.

Meanwhile, Kelly and his estranged wife Morgan are having problems, and their marriage counselor can't help. The situation is not helped by Morgan's passionate attraction to Josh. She decides she wants a divorce. Later, she tells her stunned mother, Jennifer, that

Paternity becomes an issue in Springfield. When Nola finds out that Quint is Henry Chamberlain's son, Quint is furious!

Morgan's passionate attraction to Josh means the end of her marriage to Kelly.

Mark has been having an affair with Amanda. Ultimately, Jennifer packs her bags and leaves.

But Mark's problems are not merely marital. Apparently, someone in Springfield knows he is really Samuel Pasquin! Mark's sinister associate, Bryan Lister, has been murdering people he thinks suspect Mark's true identity.

Early in March, secrets from the past are revealed. Mark confides to Amanda that he's the true heir to half of Spaulding Enterprises and is trying to regain his inheritance. And Quint tells Nola what happened ten years earlier at the archeological dig in Tanquir. The explosives Quint was responsible for setting up misfired, killing Mrs. Renfield's husband. Quint is determined to go back to Tanquir to try to learn if the accident was really his fault.

Helena also feels responsible for Professor Renfield's death and has been blackmailed about the incident all these years. Now she and Quint suspect that the explosives were intentionally set off. In Tanquir, Quint and the blackmailer are trapped in a cave-in at the site. Only Quint survives, and he's joyfully reunited with Nola, who has come to Tanquir looking for him.

Meanwhile, Mark is diving for the strongbox hidden beneath the boathouse. He now has evidence supporting his claim to Spaulding Enterprises; he also finds proof that Bryan caused Mark's father's death. In a final confrontation in the boathouse, Mark kills Bryan and convinces Amanda not to tell the police. Nevertheless he's soon arrested.

Quint and Nola return to Springfield and plan to marry. A furious Rebecca tells Nola that Quint had pushed Rebecca off a cliff, causing her disfigurement and miscarriage. Quint has blanked the whole incident out but believes her version of it. Rebecca arranges to have everyone, including Mark, brought together on a cliff to re-enact her accident. She reveals that she is really Mona Enright and that Mark is her husband—his real name: Samuel Pasquin. Also it was Mark, not Quint, who pushed her that night. Crazy Rebecca now tries to push Amanda off the cliff. Mark manages to save Amanda, but is shot by Rebecca and falls to his death. Rebecca then leaps after him, thus clearing the stage nicely for Quint's marriage to Nola. They set the date: June 24.

Quint and Nola return to Springfield and blissfully set the date for their wedding.

Bert Bauer's friendship with a dying patient leads her to set up a patients' advocacy group.

Rick and Beth play their own version of musical chairs.

Bert Bauer has involved herself with a terminally ill patient at the hospital. Her friendship and understanding help him to cope with his fear of dying. Although he does ultimately succumb to his illness, Bert works to set up a patients' advocacy group to help others like him. Hope contributes money toward it and Bert runs it.

Trish's and Josh's perky niece, Mindy, pops up in Springfield as Quint and Nola's wedding approaches. She befriends a painfully shy student, Beth Raines. Fellow students Rick and Philip become interested in both girls and soon there's a four-way romantic mix-up among the teenagers.

Vanessa throws Quint and Nola an elaborate engagement party and later Quint has a bachelor's party with his male friends. Trying to eavesdrop, Nola hides in the hollowed cake and manages to get trapped inside it. At last the wedding day arrives and everything works out—just barely. Left behind when everyone heads for the church, Nola ends up hitching a ride on a firetruck! The couple enjoys a romantic honeymoon in Ireland.

Floyd becomes engaged to Lesley Ann, who soon is smitten with the charmingly manipulative Warren. After much indecision, Floyd breaks up with her over this rival.

Hope and Alan Spaulding grow more estranged as Alan relies more and more upon Trish Lewis—even for advice on how to redecorate the house. Hope turns to alcohol for solace.

Billy Lewis and the mysterious Annabelle are disturbed by a pho-

Vanessa is the perfect hostess when she throws an elaborate engagement party for Quint and Nola.

Nola barely makes it to the church on time for her wedding to Quint!

The Spaulding family is on the rocks, especially Hope, who has turned to alcohol for comfort.

tograph that Tony's father took many years ago. Tony himself is obsessed with the picture and with Annabelle's uncanny resemblance to the young woman shown there.

Annabelle herself begins to suffer a series of blackouts, as a way of blocking memories of her past. It will be some time before the meaning of the photograph is made clear, but essentially the story is this: Twenty years ago Tom Reardon took the picture of four men and a girl—Annabelle's mother, Annie. Annie was a carefree sort with an improvisatory morality who used to swim about in the lake and befriend some of the gentlemen fishermen. The men in the picture were of this ilk, and one day, after a few drinks and one thing leading to another, she stripped off her bathing suit and demonstrated for them her skinnydipping techniques. When her suit vanished and the men left, she spotted her husband's rowboat and swam out to it. But Eli, her husband, had had enough of her ways and refused to take her aboard. Five-year-old Annabelle was also in the boat and had to watch as her mother was left behind struggling in the water. The next day the woman's body was washed to shore and Eli, to cover his guilt, murdered Tom Reardon. This, too, took place before little Annabelle's terrified eyes. You'd have blackouts, too.

And now, twenty years later, the men pictured in the photograph begin to die. Bill Bauer is one of them, and his murder is made to look like suicide. Henry Chamberlain, another of the pictured fishermen, survives repeated attempts on his life. Then Annabelle's psychiatrist, who is getting dangerously close to the secret of the girl's past, is murdered.

Tony Reardon, son of the long-ago-murdered Tom, helps his girlfriend Annabelle unravel the mystery. The clues point more and more to Eli, especially when an attempt is made on H. B. Lewis's life and Billy's car is blown up. (Billy, the intended victim, was not in the car, but his secretary was killed.) Annabelle begins remembering some details from her deep past, and Eli decides to bring her back to the lake where her mother Annie died. Once there, he admits that he killed Annie. When he takes Annabelle out in a rowboat and all the memories come flooding back, the full danger of her situation becomes clear to her. Eli then pushes her overboard and attempts to bludgeon her with an oar.

At that moment, Tony providentially appears and struggles to save Annabelle. Eli falls from the boat and presumably drowns. Later, Tony recalls hearing a rifle shot. In fact, H.B. shot Eli from land.

Meanwhile, the teen triangle of Mindy, Philip, and Beth continues to cause much hard feelings. The situation is brought to a crisis by Beth's altogether awful father, Bradley, who humiliates the girl by having a doctor examine her to confirm her virginity, and some weeks later traumatizes her by beating and raping her. Finally, she runs away, and Bradley gets a court order and sends the police to drag her back home. Beth begs Philip to help her, and the two of them run off to New York City during Christmas week. A sidewalk Santa befriends the bewildered kids, takes them in and feeds them. But somehow Bradley has tracked them down and is shadowing them.

A mysterious new character, Dr. John Stevens, runs into Hillary by chance at a mountain cabin. Immediately attracted to each other, they end up making love—without ever learning each other's names. It turns out he's been doing viral research for Alan Spaulding in South America. Spaulding has ordered him back to work at the Cedars Hospital. Katie, who becomes Dr. Stevens's secretary, quickly falls for him. Then, of course, Hillary shows up and is stunned to see the man she'd made love to at the cabin.

Mystery swirls around Tony and Annabelle. Why is he obsessed with a photograph his father took many years before, and why does Annabelle look so much like the young woman in the photo?

Profiles

Charita Bauer
(Bert Bauer)

The only original cast member still playing in *Guiding Light*, Charita Bauer joined the show in 1950, when it was a radio serial. She's continued as "Bert" ever since, growing from young aproned mother to socially concerned matriarch. "Spunk, definite point of view, doesn't mince words, very frank," that's how longtime *GL* producer Leslie Kwartin describes both Charita and the character she plays. Fifty years after her theatrical debut in the 1933 Broadway production of *Thunder on the Left*, Miss Bauer was honored by the Academy of Television Arts and Sciences with its Lifetime Achievement Award.

Christopher Bernau
(Alan Spaulding)

An actor well-remembered for his portrayal of Philip Todd in TV's *Dark Shadows*, it was only natural that in 1977 Chris Bernau would be offered the lead in off-Broadway's *The Passion of Dracula*. At the same time he was offered the role of Alan Spaulding in *GL*, so for a while he juggled both roles. The forty-four-year-old actor is known for his theater work, having toured with the national company of *Who's Afraid of Virginia Woolf?* and having appeared in the New York productions of *The Boys in the Band* and *The Real Inspector Hound*. Chris says he's a fan of all types of music, particularly opera.

Lisa Brown
(Nola Chamberlain)

Lisa Brown has certainly been in the thick of things lately. Since landing the role of Nola on *GL* in February 1980, Lisa assumed the lead in the Broadway musical, *42nd Street*, and managed to play both roles for over a year. Then in October 1982 she married her *GL* costar, Tom Nielson, and they expect a child in the spring of 1984. It's hard to imagine that even motherhood will slow down this Broadway veteran, who says she's been dancing since the age of three.

Rebecca Hollen
(Trish Lewis)

When the young, Oklahoma-born actress came to New York City a few years back, she worked as a model and began studying acting (with Mary Tarcai). Soon she was doing commercials and cohosting a cable TV talk show, *Cue on View*. She landed a recurring role on *One Life to Live* and for a year played Tina Cornell on *As the World Turns* before joining *GL* in June 1981.

Maeve Kinkead
(Vanessa Chamberlain)

Before coming to GL in 1980, Maeve Kinkead played Angie Perrini for three years on *Another World*. Before that, her experience was mainly on the stage. She studied and performed at the London Academy of Music and Dramatic Art (LAMDA) and appeared in a number of classic roles at Harvard University's Loeb Drama Center. Maeve was born in New York City and is married to the dancer-choreographer, Harry Streep. Their son, Abraham Kinkead Streep, was born October 23, 1981.

Tom Nielsen
(Floyd Parker)

A singer and songwriter as well as an actor, twenty-nine-year-old Tom Nielsen has cut several records and performed in such New York nightspots as The Bottom Line and The Lone Star Cafe. A few years ago, as an unemployed actor, he was managing an ice cream parlor in Hollywood. But then he joined the Lee Strasberg Institute and studied acting under Anna Strasberg, and eventually he began getting small, offbeat parts. He joined GL in April 1980, and two and a half years later married his GL costar, Lisa Brown (Nola). They live in New York City.

William Roerick
(Henry Chamberlain)

Born in 1912 in New Jersey, William Roerick has been primarily a stage actor, having appeared with Basil Rathbone in *The Heiress* and with Katherine Cornell in *Saint Joan*. He also played Laertes to John Gielgud's *Hamlet*. After numerous appearances in TV shows and films, Roerick joined *GL* in June 1980. In his time off, he drives up to his farm in Stockbridge, Massachusetts, where he gardens and works at carpentry.

Don Stewart
(Michael Bauer)

A man of many talents, the forty-four-year-old actor and singer has appeared in plays on and off Broadway. Back when he was twenty-four, Don was the youngest aircraft commander in the Strategic Air Command, reportedly flying some 1,800,000 miles in jet bombers. Nowadays, he lives with his wife and two children in New Jersey. In June 1983, he appeared in a musical revue, *Some Enchanted Evening*, at the Kennedy Center in Washington. He's been on *GL* since December 1968.

Michael Tylo
(Quinton Chamberlain)

Thirty-five-year-old Michael Tylo earned his master's degree in theater at Wayne State University, where he became involved in a local repertory group. Since then, he has worked with The Theatre in Detroit, the Dearborn (Michigan) Repertory, and the Long Wharf Theatre. In 1982, he appeared with *GL* costar Jerry ver Dorn in *The Star-Spangled Girl* at the Playhouse on the Mall (Paramus, New Jersey). A *GL* cast member since September 1981, Michael is married to actress Deborah Eckols.

Jerry ver Dorn
(Ross Marler)

A *GL* cast member since 1979, Jerry ver Dorn was born in Sioux Falls, South Dakota, in 1949. He studied theater at Moorehead State University in Minnesota, as well as in London. Later he appeared in Eric Bentley's play, *Are You Now or Have You Ever Been?* which eventually made it to Broadway. In 1982, Jerry and his wife Beth reorganized the Playhouse on the Mall (Paramus, New Jersey) and presented a season of plays. He himself writes plays, and professes a love for crossword puzzles.

Arrivals and Departures

Warren Burton
(Warren Andrews)

The first acting job for Chicago-born Warren Burton was the part of Tulsa in the touring company of *Gypsy*, with Ann Southern. He then came to New York and joined the original off-Broadway production of *Hair*. Particularly valuable were the two years he spent working at the New York nightclub, Upstairs at the Downstairs, where he did a variety of tasks including writing and performing comedy. Since then he's written material for Lily Tomlin and appeared in three of her TV specials. In 1980, while playing nasty Eddie Dorrance on *All My Children*, Warren was awarded an Emmy for outstanding supporting actor. He has since worked on *Another World* (as Jason Dunlap) and in May 1983 joined the cast of *Guiding Light*.

Judi Evans
(Beth Raines)

Young, slim, single, blonde, blue-eyed— Judi Evans is a vivid new presence on *Guiding Light*. Her parents worked in a circus and at age two Judi became a circus clown, a part she played until she was eight. Later she attended Pasadena City College, where she studied acting. She modeled, worked in TV commercials, and appeared in a Dom DeLuise TV special before originating the role of Beth Raines on *GL* in May 1983.

Jennifer Cooke
(Morgan Nelson)

Twenty-year-old Jennifer Cooke left *Guiding Light* in spring 1983, after a year and a half on the show. She began working in commercials at the age of nine and is said to have done more than two hundred of them. She has also appeared in several TV movies, including *Tom and Joanne*, in which she played Elizabeth Ashley's daughter.

Geraldine Court
(Jennifer Evans)

Soap and stage veteran Geraldine Court left *Guiding Light* this spring after three years on the show. Previously, she'd had roles on *The Doctors* (1972–77), *As The World Turns*, and *Another World*. She toured Europe in 1977 with the LaMama Experimental Theatre Company, in the plays *The Trojan Women* and *As You Like It*. She and four fellow actors have recently formed their own theater company, the Future Directors Theatre.

Kathleen Cullen
(Amanda Spaulding)

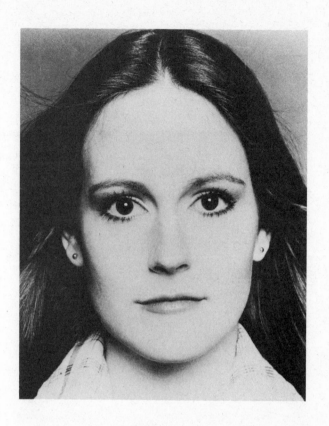

Kathleen Cullen left *Guiding Light* in 1983 after five years as Amanda, her first TV role. She came to New York from Illinois in 1976 to study acting at the Herbert Berghof Studios and dance at the American Dance Center. She also studied acting in London and while there starred in *A Midsummer Night's Dream* and *The Sea*. Back in New York, she was soon appearing in numerous off-Broadway productions.

Leslie O'Hara
(Rebecca Cartwright)

In her fairly brief reign on *Guiding Light* (Rebecca was gloriously killed off early in 1983), Leslie O'Hara made the most of a juicy role. She studied drama in England, appearing in repertory productions of *Under Milk Wood*, *She Stoops to Conquer*, and *The Importance of Being Earnest*. More recently she played in an off-Broadway production of *Beside the Seaside*. She has studied drama with Stella Adler and dance with Alvin Ailey.

Mark Pinter
(Mark Evans)

The Iowa-born actor left *GL* in the spring at the culmination of a highly dramatic storyline. Soap opera buffs may remember Pinter's earlier role as Dr. Tom Crawford on *Love of Life*. He's also appeared in the TV dramas, *The Secrets of Midland Heights* and *Behind the Screen*. Mark lives with his wife, actress Gretchen De Boer, and their three-year-old daughter, Siri.

Thomas O'Rourke
(Dr. Justin Marler)

Tom O'Rourke left *GL* after nearly eight years as Dr. Marler (his first major daytime role). In the past he's done a great deal of work in regional and off-Broadway theater, including *Endicott and the Red Cross*, *Waiting for Lefty*, and *Night*. The blond, six-foot-four-inch actor is also proficient at fencing, horseback riding, and photography. He is married to actress-model Marcy Casterline.

Susan Pratt
(Dr. Claire Ramsey)

Born in Florida, Susan Pratt moved to New York at the age of ten, when her father was hired as a newscaster by WCBS-TV. After high school, Susan worked for a year in Paris, traveled to Munich, then came back to enroll in the American Academy of Dramatic Arts. The spontaneous actress then packed for Los Angeles, where she eventually landed the role of Annie Logan on *General Hospital*. She joined *GL* in July 1983.

James Rebhorn
(Bradley Raines)

The tall, Philadelphia-born actor earned his M.F.A. degree at Columbia University and went on to appear with nearly every major off-Broadway theater company, including the New York Shakespeare Festival (in *Othello*). After playing recurring roles on *The Doctors* and *Texas*, Jim joined the cast of *GL* in May 1983. He devotes his free time to Imagination Workshop, a drama program for the mentally ill, at Mt. Sinai Hospital in New York.

Elvera Roussel
(Hope Spaulding)

New York-born Elvera Roussel traveled extensively in the Far East, Germany, and Africa as a young girl, then spent her teen years on Long Island, New York. She studied theater at Hofstra University and was soon appearing in numerous regional productions, including *The Glass Menagerie* and *The Lion in Winter*. Elvera joined *GL* in March 1979, leaving the show in late fall of 1983. Before leaving, she appeared in the 1983 CBS TV movie, *The Cradle Will Fall*, as her *GL* character, Hope Spaulding. The multi-talented actress also writes screenplays and will soon produce an independent film called *Kisses*.

Krista Tesreau
(Mindy Lewis)

Young Krista Tesreau joined *Guiding Light* in May 1983 in the role of teenager Mindy Lewis. Besides being an actress, Krista is also an accomplished pianist, winner of a Jefferson City, Missouri, concerto competition, as well as the nationwide Liberace Talent Search. She has also found time (and talent and looks) to win the Miss T.E.E.N. pageant for the state of Missouri and was recently featured in a *Seventeen* magazine article, "Talented Teenagers."

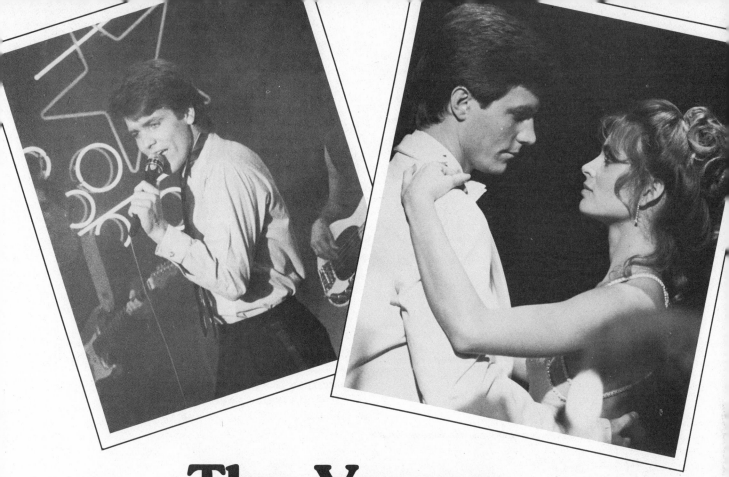

The Young and the Restless

CBS

The Cast

Deborah Adair (left
in fall) .... *Jill Foster Abbott*

Marla Adams (new in
April) .... *Dina Abbott Mergeron*

Meg Bennett .... *Julia Newman*

Eric Braeden .... *Victor Newman*

Tracey Bregman (new
in spring) .... *Lauren Fenmore*

Robert Colbert (left
in fall) .... *Stuart Brooks*

Carolyn
Conwell .... *Mary Williams*

Jeanne Cooper ..... *Katherine Chancellor*

Michael
Damian............. *Danny Romalotti*

Doug Davidson...... *Paul Williams*

Eileen Davidson ..... *Ashley Abbott*

Kristine de Bell (left
early in year) ..... *Pam Warren*

Brenda Dickson
(started in
fall) .... *Jill Foster Abbott*

Alex Donnelley ...... *Diane Jenkins*

Jerry Douglas........ *John Abbott*

Michael Evans .... *Douglas Austin*

Andrea Evans-
Massey (new in
spring) .... *Patti Williams Abbott*

Steven Ford .... *Andy Richards*

Velekka Gray (new   *Dr. Sharon Reaves/*
in May) .... *Ruby Collins*

Brett Hadley.......... *Carl Williams*

Ben Hammer (late
spring only) .... *Alex Morgan*

Christopher
Holder .... *Kevin Bancroft*

Randy Holland (new
in spring) .... *Rick Daros*

Jay Kerr (left early in
1983).............. *Brian Forbes*

Terry Lester........... *Jack Abbott*

Beth Maitland........ *Traci Abbott*

Margaret Mason (in
spring only) .... *Eve*

Brian Matthews (new
in February)....... *Eric Garrison*

Julianna
McCarthy .... *Elizabeth Foster Brooks*

Scott Palmer (new in
spring)............. *Prof. Tim Sullivan*

Brock Peters.......... *Frank Lewis*

Marguerite Ray...... *Mamie*

DeAnna Robbins (left
early in year) ..... *Cindy Lake*

Jon St. Elwood (new
in spring) .... *Jazz*

Lilibet Stern (left
early in year) ..... *Patti Williams Abbott*

Carl Strano (in spring
only) .... *Max*

Mark Tapscott (left
early in year) ..... *Earl Bancroft*

Joseph Taylor (on in
Janurary, off in
spring)............. *Tony DiSalvo*

Christopher
Templeton (new in
spring)............. *Carol Robbins*

Melody Thomas...... *Nikki Reed Bancroft*

Patty Weaver .... *Gina Roma*

Stephanie E. Williams
(new in
January)........... *Amy Lewis*

Lynn Wood .... *Alison Bancroft*

Creators: *William J. Bell and Lee Phillip
Bell*

**Executive
Producers:** *William J. Bell, H. Wesley Kenney*

Producer: *Edward Scott*

**Associate
Producer:** *Tom Langan*

Directors: *Frank Pacelli, Rudy Vejar, Dennis
Steinmetz*

Writers: *William J. Bell; with Kay Alden,
Meg Bennett, Elizabeth
Harrower, Randy Holland, Eric
Roberts, John F. Smith, Sally
Sussman*

Background

The Young and the Restless, which marked its tenth anniversary on March 26, 1983, has a glossier, more glamorous feel to it than many of the other soaps. It may be set in the fictional Midwest community of Genoa City, but it makes you think: California (which is, in fact, where it is taped). Filled with attractive, young, musically talented characters, fancy sets, and storylines that interweave the sexy with the sinister, *Y&R* focusses particularly on the fortunes of the Abbotts, the Bancrofts, and the Williamses. There's the Jabot Cosmetics enterprise, headed by John Abbott, whose three grown children, Jack, Ashley, and Traci, raise various kinds of hell. There's ex-police lieutenant Carl Williams, whose son Paul is working undercover, infiltrating the crime syndicate in hopes of clearing his dad's name. Finally, there's Earl Bancroft, whose daughter-in-law, Nikki, is a striptease artist. Nikki's baby daughter, Victoria, is not the child of her husband, Kevin Bancroft, but of a Genoa City business tycoon, Victor Newman. In all, it's a wonderfully volatile mix of characters, and the stories in which they're involved are exciting and fast-paced, even when they strain credibility just a bit.

The Story

The year starts off with a striptease by Nikki, who's performing in The Bayou to save the foundering club. When her husband Kevin finds out, he's outraged, but she refuses to quit her trade. Jill, plotting to steal her husband John Abbott's money, has his son Jack's office bugged. Listening in as Jack and Diane rendezvous in the office, Jill gets Jack's pregnant wife Patti to visit him at work. Patti hurries to the office, sees Jack in another woman's arms, and blindly rushes out. She falls down, is taken to the hospital, and loses the baby.

"Victor Newman must be killed." Julia overhears this much on the phone and warns Victor that he's in danger. Eve and her penniless fiance, Max, are behind the murder plot and manage to administer to Victor a dose of a drug that could eventually kill him and leave no trace in the bloodstream.

Alison confronts Victor with "proof" that Victoria was fathered by him, but he denies everything. Eventually Alison comes to believe that baby Victoria is a true Bancroft.

The new Jabot fragrance, "Julia," is finally introduced at a press party to which Ashley and Brian have not been invited. They're further infuriated when Jack takes full credit for the fragrance. Jack wants his father to sell Jabot to another company, Mergeron, thus improving everyone's cash flow. He also wants to bring in Mergeron's Eric Garrison to replace Ashley's current love, Brian. Jack's father, John, is violently opposed to the plan, and after numerous dirty tricks and a tempestuous confrontation with his son, John suffers a heart attack. His wife Jill worries about the open-heart surgery he must then undergo, but she can't help thinking of the millions she stands to inherit if he dies. Ultimately, he recovers.

Meanwhile, the syndicate finds out about Paul's and Cindy's undercover investigation and a contract is put out on them. Paul's apartment is blown up, but he and Cindy escape. Paul confides in the only man he can trust on the police force, Alex Morgan, not realizing that Alex himself is working for the syndicate. To force Paul to come out of hiding, the syndicate kidnaps his mother, Mary Williams. After much lurking and skulking, a horse stampede, and a shootout, Mary is saved from the clutches of the criminals. The Williamses are reunited, and Paul's father Carl is cleared of criminal charges and welcomed back onto the force. It's somewhat more difficult for Carl and Mary to accept Paul's love, Cindy, who used to be a prostitute.

Although Patti is back with Jack, he's up to his young tricks again, this time with Diane. Victor continues to languish as Eve and Max keep administering his daily dose of poison. Julia, not trusting Eve,

After John has a heart attack, son Jack and wife Jill wait for news.

sneaks in and discovers a nearly dead Victor. She becomes convinced that Eve has been poisoning him. Lab analysis proves the validity of her suspicions, and the efficacy of an antidote. Victor is told of all this, and he vows revenge, especially when he learns Eve's murder motive: that her son might inherit half of John's estate.

The revenge is, to say the least, a confusing bit of business. Victor will propose to Eve, then feign death in order to draw her out into the open. She quickly accepts his proposal (dumping Max) and on the eve of the wedding is shocked to hear that he has died. A funeral is held and Victor (hidden) is moved to realize how many people care about him. Indeed Nikki is quite distraught, blaming herself for his demise. Eve is terrified when Julia announces she thinks Victor's death is suspicious and plans to have his body exhumed. Disguised, Max sneaks back to dig up Victor's body before an autopsy can be performed. Eve is shocked when she sees Victor's "ghost," and she soon shows signs of losing her mind. She wheels in Victor's casket as a witness when she marries Max! The casket is opened and found to be empty, so Max knocks Eve unconscious and dumps her in the casket for safekeeping. If you've followed this so far, you won't be surprised to learn that Victor suddenly appears and that during the subsequent struggle with him Max falls against a pitchfork and dies. Eve is shipped off to a mental hospital to sort things out.

Traci, meanwhile, very nearly goes off her diet when nasty Lauren sends a banana split to her table. Traci has a stronger self-image now than before and dumps the untouched gooey goodness over Lauren's head. She's determined to lose weight and not lose Danny Romalotti.

Lauren tries to sabotage Traci's diet by sending her a banana split, but Traci wisely puts it on Lauren's head rather than in her own stomach.

Traci is determined not to lose Danny to that vixen-in-training Lauren.

Nikki the stripper has marital problems with Kevin and is drawn to Rick, who's been doing his worst to seduce her. And Jack and Ashley get a shock when the mysterious Madame Mergeron shows up to buy out Jabot Cosmetics and turns out to be none other than their mother, Dina Abbott, who'd walked out on them twelve years

Things really get confusing when Madame Mergeron turns out to be Dina Abbott. What's going on here?

before. Dina's reappearance throws everything into confusion, including the status of Jill's marriage to John Abbott.

John's son Jack is having some problems of his own when his wife Patti overhears him making an appointment to have a vasectomy. She realizes he married her only to guarantee that he'd get to be president of Jabot Cosmetics. Distraught, she buys a gun, shows up at Jack's office and threatens to shoot herself. At the last moment she shows good sense and shoots him instead.

During surgery, two bullets are removed from Jack's chest, but a third remains. Jack is paralyzed and Patti has no recollection of having shot him. (Amnesia strikes again in soapland!) A second dangerous operation cures the paralysis. Patti starts seeing a psychiatrist.

Nikki has now decided to divorce Kevin, and he goes along with the idea. Soon Kevin is getting helpful hints on the single life from Julia, and a friendship is born. Nikki turns to Rick for solace. Alison, meanwhile, plans to betray Nikki in order to win custody of little Victoria. She has a film of Nikki's strip act, which has been doctored to make it look like a real porno movie. Its title: *Hot Hips.* That should make effective evidence in a custody fight.

Nikki has given Kevin nothing but trouble, so it's no surprise when he agrees to her plans for a divorce.

Nikki plots to get the tape back from the mobster who made it. He agrees to let her have it—if she'll marry him. She says all right but secretly hopes to get out of it.

Amy, Paul, and Andy manage to capture Jazz and get him to the detective's office, where Jazz confirms that Tony DiSalvo is out to get them all. Just then, Tony pulls a switch that traps Andy, Paul and Jazz in the office. Then gas is pumped in. Luckily Cindy comes by and saves them.

Jazz saves the day when he shoots mobster Tony DiSalvo.

At Sleazy's Bar, Tony's wedding to Nikki is about to take place. Suddenly Andy and Paul appear. Tony gets the drop on them. Cindy barges in and gets shot, but before Tony can shoot again Jazz sneaks up and shoots the mobster dead.

Jack is recovering from being shot by Patti. When she visits him, he gently assures her that he'll be a better husband to her. Her eyes brim with tears and they embrace. It soon becomes impossible to hide from the police the fact that Patti had fired the shots, even though she has blocked out all memory of doing so. Her psychiatrist tells Jack that to break that block they must recreate the original stress situation under controlled circumstances. They even provide a gun for her—but load it with blanks. Unfortunately, she goes out and buys a gun of her own, filled with live ammunition. The re-enactment of the situation takes place—including Jack's remark about getting a vasectomy—and Patti very nearly shoots him again. At the last moment, she does not. But her clear memory of the past produces a very different, and stronger, Patti. Realizing how Jack had manipulated her, she tells him that they ought to call off their relationship.

Danny, on hearing about this separation, runs to be with Patti; but she knows he's about to become engaged to scheming Lauren and doesn't encourage him to get close.

During Jack's recuperation, his sister Ashley has taken over his duties as president of Jabot; and she's been doing such a smashing job that John Abbott asks her to stay on permanently. Jack is demoted to director of advertising. It is a crushing blow, coming right after his loss of Patti.

Baby Victoria has been staying with Alison Bancroft, Nikki's ex-mother-in-law, in San Francisco. Alison promises to bring the child back to Genoa City right away, now that Nikki's problems with Tony are over. But in reality, she leaves the country with Victoria and plans to be gone for years.

Nikki is frantic when she realizes her daughter has been kidnapped, and she even goes on television to beg Alison to return the child. Rick, meanwhile, has a hunch. He'd heard Alison speak wistfully about a little town in England called Appleshaw, and he flies over there. Sure enough, he finds her. Confronting her, he says she has no right to that child, because her son, Kevin, is not the father; Victor Newman is! Stunned to hear that she is not the baby's grandmother, Alison does not resist when Rick takes the baby back to the States.

Nikki is absolutely ecstatic at Victoria's return. Rick quickly proposes to her, but she's had bad luck at marriage. She agrees to live with him for a while, though, to see if that works. And so they do, and soon find that they get along extremely well. Once again, Victor Newman holds himself back from telling Nikki that he's her child's father.

Ashley, for all her spectacular success at Jabot, is having trouble landing the man she loves, Eric Garrison. The trouble is her mother, Dina, who also has been having an affair with Eric and will do anything to avoid losing him. But her young glamorous daughter is impossibly tough competition, and Eric has made his choice. The tricky part, though, is that Ashley doesn't know about the affair Eric had with Dina.

She finds out in an unfortunate way: Dina offers to help her daughter and Eric with their wedding plans, and when Eric's things arrive from Paris she makes sure his portrait of herself is prominently among them. Naturally Ashley asks him about the picture. Then she sees the inscription on the back: "All my love, Eric."

Ashley is shocked at the revelation, and Eric, at least, does not

It's all in the family when Eric has an affair with both Dina and Ashley. Ashley wins his hand, but Dina will do anything to sabotage their wedding plans.

resort to lies. He does, however, later give Dina a royal dressing down for her "deliberate, cruel act." Indeed, Dina may have succeeded temporarily in jeopardizing Ashley's marriage plans, but she has probably forever alienated the man she loves.

But then, intergenerational rivalry is not uncommon in the world of soaps. It begins to seem, in fact, that John and his son Jack are turning into rivals over Jill. Jill had faked a pregnancy to impress John; but then, after a mishap, Jack saves her life and spends a snowy night making love to her in a cabin in the woods. Come to think of it, cabins in the woods are a common commodity in soaps as well.

And so, inevitably, are drugs. Alas, Traci's weight problem has turned into a drug problem and late in 1983 she nearly overdoses, crashes her car, and ends in the hospital. Danny's reaction, extreme loving concern for Traci, arouses Lauren's jealousy, but there's nothing she can do about it.

Hearing about her sister's accident and hospitalization, Ashley rushes to Traci's bedside just as Traci goes into convulsions. Soon the girl comes out of it, and a worried and weary Ashley lets her rest. In the waiting room, Ashley runs into Eric, and forgetting her jealousy, she embraces him.

Meg Bennett
(Julia Newman)

The beautiful brunette actress played Julia on *Y&R* from January 1980 until June 1981, when her character got a divorce and whisked off to Paris to open a fashion boutique. She rejoined the serial in September 1982, when Jabot Cosmetics enticed Julia back to endorse a new line of fragrances. California-born Meg graduated from the Theater Department at Northwestern University and began performing in several stock productions, including *Picnic, Mame,* and *Cabaret.* She was in the original off-Broadway production of *Godspell* and for two and a half years played in the original Broadway production of *Grease.* Coming to soapland, Meg played Liza for three years on *Search* before joining *Y&R*, where she not only acts the part of Julia, but also writes dialogue for the show.

Eric Braeden
(Victor Newman)

Born Hans Gudegast in the Baltic port city of Kiel, Eric came to the U.S. on a track-and-field scholarship to study at Montana State University. After a year there, the adventurous youngster braved the tumultuous Salmon River in Idaho in a small boat. He and his partner were the first persons ever to do so. They made a film of their exploits and went to Hollywood to find someone to distribute it. Instead, it was Eric who got distributed, acting in over one hundred and twenty television programs during the past two decades. He joined *The Young and the Restless* in January 1980 and was honored as best new daytime star in the Eleventh Annual Daytime TV Magazine Reader's Poll. The athletic actor lives in Los Angeles with his wife, Dale, and their son, Christian.

Robert Colbert
(Stuart Brooks)

An original cast member of *Y&R*, Robert Colbert got his start in show business while serving in the Army in Okinawa. He was tapped for a role in an Air Force Special Services production of *The Caine Mutiny*. Returning to the States, he took a screen test and was put under contract to Warner Brothers and began appearing frequently on the *Maverick* series. He later worked under contract for Universal and 20th-Century-Fox. The tall (six-foot-two) actor has brown eyes and salt-and-pepper hair and lives in Santa Monica, California. In his spare time, he rides motorcycles and flies airplanes.

Michael Damian
(Danny Romalotti)

Michael Damian was just nineteen and had never acted before when he undertook the role of Danny on *Y&R* in June 1981. The second youngest of nine children, Michael grew up in a musical family—his mother is a concert pianist. All the children in the family learned to play at least three instruments. Michael and his older brother Larry have written songs which Michael has sung on *Y&R*. The blue-eyed, five-foot-ten-inch actor lives in Los Angeles with his family. He was recently an honorary chairman of the March of Dimes "Walk-America" walkathon.

Doug Davidson
(Paul Williams)

The California-born six-footer left college before graduating in order to pursue his acting career. He took acting classes and auditioned during the days and worked nights as a cab driver, waiter, and bartender. Soon he began getting work in commercials, which in turn led to parts in the film *Fraternity Row* and the TV movie *The Initiation of Sarah*. Doug joined *Y&R* in February 1980, and in his spare time he camps, water-skis, writes songs, and plays the bagpipes.

Eileen Davidson
(Ashley Abbott)

The tall, blonde-haired, green-eyed actress definitely has that California girl look. Impatient to get started with her career, she left college and began modeling. Soon she was making commercials in Europe, appearing in plays (e.g., *In the Boom Boom Room* and *Born Yesterday*), and landing parts in such films as *The House on Sorority Row* and *Goin' All the Way*. She joined *Y&R* in June 1982.

Steven Ford
(Andy Richards)

The third son of former President Gerald Ford grew up in Alexandria, Virginia, and later studied animal sciences at California State Polytechnic University. Two years of that were enough and Ford headed to California, where he got a part in a movie called *Cattle Annie and Little Britches*. He decided acting was all right and soon appeared in the film *Escape from New York,* as well as in several TV shows. He joined the cast of *Y&R* in June 1981. He spends his free time riding the horses he keeps on his thirteen-acre ranch.

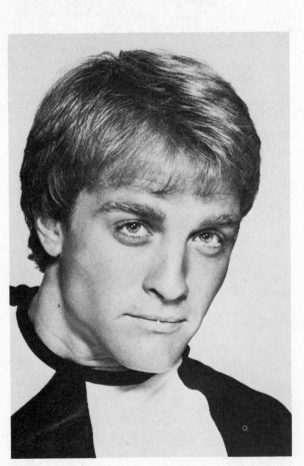

Terry Lester
(Jack Abbott)

The Indiana-born actor earned his B.A. degree in political science, but he was always interested in theater and played in a number of summer stock productions (including *Hello, Dolly!* with Betty Grable) before enlisting in the Army. While serving in Washington, D.C., Terry worked in commercials in his free time. When *Airport '75* was being filmed nearby, he was fortunate enough to snag a speaking part. Upon leaving the Army, he headed out to Los Angeles to pursue an acting career. He appeared in a 1975 Lily Tomlin TV special and in several TV movies before joining *Y&R* in July 1980.

Beth Maitland
(Traci Abbott)

Beth Maitland has really caught the public's fancy (and empathy) in her role as Traci, the slightly pudgy sister of svelte Ashley. Beth was born in South Dakota and studied music theater at Arizona State College in Tempe. In Arizona and later in California she appeared in a number of theater productions, including *Man of La Mancha* and *The Miracle Worker*. Her idol is Jimmy Stewart, whose middle name she chose for her surname. She joined *The Young and the Restless* in June 1982.

Julianna McCarthy
(Elizabeth Foster Brooks)

A charter member of the *Y&R* cast, the silver-haired Julianna grew up in Pennsylvania and made her stage debut at the age of fifteen. Later, she majored in drama at the University of Iowa and went on to play in the Broadway production of *Inherit the Wind*. During the 1960s, she gave up her career in favor of motherhood (she has a daughter, Thea, and a son, Brendan); but in 1971, following a divorce, she began appearing on TV series such as *The Bold Ones* and *Dr. Kildare*. Julianna lives with her children and several pets in L.A.'s San Fernando Valley.

Brock Peters
(Frank Lewis)

The intensity of Brock Peter's acting style has been admired at least as far back as 1963, when he won a Golden Globe Award for his part in *To Kill a Mockingbird*. Since then he has appeared in such films as *The Pawnbroker*, *Porgy and Bess*, and *Carmen Jones*. On Broadway, he appeared in *The Great White Hope* and in *Lost in the Stars* (for which he received a Tony nomination, the Outer Critics Circle Award, and the Drama Desk Award for best actor). In June 1982 Brock joined *Y&R* as Genoa City's tough police commander, Frank Lewis.

Melody Thomas
(Nikki Reed Bancroft)

Since February 1979, young Melody has played the popular role of Nikki on *Y&R*, but by then she was already quite a veteran, having worked in commercials since the age of three. Her first film role, when she was eight, was in Alfred Hitchcock's *Marnie*. Since then, the blonde Californian has appeared in seven other films and many TV shows, including *The Waltons*, in which she has a recurring role. The five-foot-five actress spends much of her spare time roller skating and adding to her extensive Barbie Doll collection.

Arrivals and Departures

Marla Adams
(Dina Abbott Mergeron)

Young Marla Adams, who joined *Y&R* in April 1983, won a number of beauty pageants while growing up in Ocean City, New Jersey, and became first runner-up in the Miss New Jersey contest. Soon she moved to New York City to study acting at the American Academy of Dramatic Arts. In fairy tale fashion her first audition landed her in the Broadway production of *The Visit.* On TV, she's made appearances on a number of shows and for six years played the role of Belle on *Secret Storm.* The blonde, green-eyed actress lives—swims, sings, paints, collects antiques—in Santa Monica, California.

Andrea Evans-Massey
(Patti Williams Abbott)

Blessed with a bushel of reddish blonde hair, Andrea is interested in music as well as acting, and after graduating from the University of Illinois went on the American Conservatory of Music in Chicago. She appeared in several stage plays and in the TV miniseries, *The Awakening Land,* and soon found herself in the role of Tina Clayton on *One Life to Live,* where she stayed four years. She joined the cast of *Y&R* in the spring of 1983, replacing Lilibet Stern in the role of Patti.

Velekka Gray
(Dr. Sharon Reaves/Ruby Collins)

At the age of thirteen, Velekka went professional, making local TV and radio commericials in her native New Orleans. Singing and modeling engagements soon followed, as well as an acting apprenticeship with the New Orleans Repertory Company. After landing the lead in the movie, *Night of Bloody Horror,* she left college, married, and headed to Hollywood, where she landed other film and TV roles. Soon the world of daytime drama engulfed her, including roles on *Love Is a Many-Splendored Thing, Somerset, Love of Live,* and *As the World Turns.* She joined *Y&R* in the spring of 1983. The honey-blonde actress is a member of Mensa, collects paperweights, and studies Chinese astrology.

Lilibet Stern
(Patti Williams Abbott)

Lilibet left *Y&R* early in 1983 after two years on the show. An accomplished singer and dancer, she taped a series of disco specials in Mexico City in 1979–80 and still hopes to become a Las Vegas headliner. In the meantime she has kept exceptionally fit working out and teaching calisthenics in Los Angeles. She appeared in the film, *The Lucifer Complex,* with Robert Vaughn, and in her free time likes to ride horses and write poetry.

Another World

NBC

HAPPY 19th ANNIVERSARY
ANOTHER WORLD

The Cast

William Andrews (in
spring only).......... George Fenton

Lewis Arlt (joined in
fall)................... David Thatcher

Christine Baranski (in
fall only) .... Beverly Tucker

Evalyn Baron .... Miss Devon

Richard Bekins (left in
spring) .... Jamie Frame

Dawn Benz (in spring
only).................. Sally Frame

Jack Betts (left in
February) .... Louis St. George

Gail Brown.............. Clarice Ewing

Danielle Burns.......... Nancy McGowan

Reggie Rock
Bythewood (left in
spring) .... R.J. Morgan

Alan Campbell (in
spring only).......... Evan Grant

David Canary (left
early in year)......... Steven Frame

Josh Clark (in summer
only).................. Bert Keller

Drew Coburn (came
and left in
spring) .... Barry Durrell

David Combs .... Sgt. Bill Gorman

Irene Dailey .... Liz Matthews

Linda Dano (started in
January).............. Felicia Gallant

Randy Danson (August
and September
only).................. Miss Rose

Terry Davis.............. Stacey Winthrop

Dillon Evans (in spring
only).................. Reginald Fearing

Geoffrey Ewing   Dist. Atty. Adam
(started in fall) .... Banks

Jose Ferrer (left in
February) .... Reuben Marino

Constance Ford......... Ada Hobson

Faith Ford .... Julia Shearer

Tisha M. Ford (left in
summer) .... Mary Sue Morgan

Nancy Frangione .... Cecile dePoulignac

Elizabeth Franz (left in
  summer) .... *Alma Rudder*
Mark Frazer (in spring
  only)................... *Prince*
Morgan Freeman .... *Roy Bingham*
Gordon Gould (August
  and September
  only)................... *Haywood*
Kim Morgan Greene
  (started early in
  year) .... *Nicole Love*
Carmine Grey .... *Cory Ewing*
Harriet Harris .... *Cathy Harris*
Jackee Harry........... *Lily Mason*
Benjamin Hendrickson
  (May to July
  only)................... *Sgt. Bartlett*
Lise Hilboldt
  (September and
  October only) .... *Janet Singleton*
Patricia Hodges........ *Maisie*
John Hutton .... *Peter Love*
Linda C. Jones (early
  spring only)........... *Rita Kent*
Charles Keating
  (started in late
  December) .... *Carl Hutchins*
Mary Page Keller
  (started in June) ..... *Sally Frame*
Anne Kerry (in spring
  only)................... *Janet Singleton*
Dana Klaboe........... *Amanda Cory*
Philip Kraus (January to
  October).............. *Mr. Barrows*
Michael LaGuardia
  (February to
  March) .... *Cullen*
Sophia Landon (joined
  in fall) .... *Jennifer Thatcher*
Jonna Lee (summer
  only)................... *Julia Shearer*
Melissa Luciano........ *Jeanne Ewing*
Laura Malone .... *Blaine Cory*
Carmen Mathews (in
  fall only) .... *Bess Killworth*
Maeve McGuire........ *Elena dePoulignac*
Betty Miller (came in
  spring, left in
  fall).................... *Jeanne Ewing*
Michael Minor.......... *Dr. Royal Dunning*
Joe Morton .... *Dr. Abel Marsh/
                          Leo Mars*
Peg Murray (early
  spring only).......... *Ada Hobson*
Gretchen Oehler........ *Vivien Gorrow*

David Oliver............. *Perry Hutchins*
Petronia Paley.......... *Quinn Harding*
Alexander Perker .... *Matthew Cory*
Lenka Peterson......... *Marie Fenton*
Richard J. Porter .... *Larry Ewing*
Joyce Reehling (in
  spring only).......... *Linda Taggert*
Luke Reilly .... *Ted Bancroft*
Christopher Rich .... *Sandy Cory*
Trevor Richards......... *Kevin Thatcher*
Kaitlin Roark............ *Maggie Cory*
Jennifer Runyon (left
  early in year)........ *Sally Frame*
Stephen Schnetzer...... *Cass Winthrop*
Nicole Schrank (left in
  early fall) .... *Maggie Cory*
Kyra Sedgwick (left in
  midyear).............. *Julia Shearer*
John Seitz (began in
  spring, left in fall).... *Zack Hill*
Michele Shay........... *Henrietta Morgan*
Craig Sisler (during
  spring only)........... *Alan Lewis*
Lois Smith .... *Ella Fitz*
Sheila Spencer......... *Thomasina Harding*
Paul Stevens............. *Brian Bancroft*
Anna Stuart (started in
  January).............. *Donna Love*
Kristine Thatcher (late
  summer to late fall).. *Miss Steiner*
Robin Thomas (joined in
  spring) .... *Mark Singleton*
Thomas Toner (during
  summer only)........ *Horace Bakewell*
Douglass Watson .... *Mackenzie Cory*
Tom Wiggin (started in
  January).............. *Gil Fenton*
Kate Wilkinson (in
  spring only).......... *Mrs. Franklin*
Victoria Wyndham...... *Rachel Davis*
Stephen Yates (took
  over part last
  summer) .... *Jamie Frame*

Executive
Producer: *Allen M. Potter (replacing Paul Rauch)*
Senior
Producer: *Mary S. Bonner*
Producer: *Kathlyn Chambers*
Associate
Producer: *Karen Stevens*
Head
writers: *Roberd Soderberg, Dorothy
          Ann Purser*
Directors: *Ira Cirker, Barnet Kellman, Ron
            Lagomarsino*

Background

Three Sally Frames, two Maggie Corys, two Jamie Frames, two Janet Singletons and three Julia Shearers mark 1983 as a year of flux among some major characters on NBC's *Another World*. NBC's daytime ratings problems may have something to do with this shifting about. Another contributing factor was the replacement of executive producer Paul Rauch with Allen M. Potter (who had been the original producer of the show). As a sort of vitamin B shot for the show's ratings, Potter steered four characters toward a double wedding. On August 4, Mackenzie (Mac) and Sandy Cory (father and son) married the women they loved (Rachel and Blaine) in a spectacular affair. Interestingly, both of these women used to be villainesses before they met their men (and their match) but have since become much more sympathetic.

And so *Another World* puts another year behind it, having come nearly to the two-decade mark (the show premiered May 4, 1964, expanding to an hour in January 1975). The six-time Emmy-winning serial is set in Bay City, U.S.A., and has come to involve high-powered politics, journalistic muckraking, the construction industry, assassination attempts, a slick bestselling authoress (coolly played by Linda Dano), as well as one of the stronger black storylines on daytime TV. The show runs the social gamut from the wealthy Loves to the middle-class Ewings to the poverty-stricken Fentons, all of them served up in a bouillabaisse of lust, jealousy, and ambition.

The Story

Love has come to Bay City—Peter Love, Nicole Love, Donna Love, and Donna's handsome chauffeur, Gil Fenton. At the same time a 1982 art scam storyline winds up in a shootout and the arrest of Cecile's father Louis. Sandy is revealed to have been an undercover agent, not one of the conspirators as greedy Cecile had believed. Her dad, Louis, in very hot water, fights extradition to France, and Cecile starts a custody battle with Sandy over their daughter, Maggie. There's a financial aspect to the fight, since Maggie's guardian stands to receive a substantial income from Louis's Swiss account. When Sandy is awarded custody, an enraged Cecile announces that he isn't the girl's father; Jamie Frame is! Sandy balks

Cecile and Louis definitely need a lawyer. He's fighting extradition to France and she's waging a custody battle. Jose Ferrer guest stars as legal counsel.

Mac will do anything to be near Rachel. When she's hospitalized after a car accident, he disguises himself as a visiting hospital administrator.

at taking a blood test that might prove or disprove his paternity.

Steve Frame and Rachel, meanwhile, have broken up, gotten back together, and become engaged; but on their way to their Key West wedding they have a terrible accident which kills Steve and leaves Rachel temporarily blind. During her lengthy recovery, she sends her daughter Amanda to live with Mac Cory, who is devoted to them both. In order to remain near Rachel, Mac pretends to be a visiting hospital administrator named John Caldwell. The ruse is necessary because Rachel doesn't want Mac's sympathy, and in any case is not ready to return the love he has always felt for her. Only later, when her sight returns and she wants to live again, does she begin to feel love for Mac. Before long, the two become engaged.

Cass Winthrop, meanwhile, has plans to start his own publishing firm and tries to lure (in fact, seduce) bestselling author Felicia Gallant away from Cory Publishing.

Beautiful Quinn Harding gets Gil a job at Frame-Harding Construction, where he soon proves his worth by saving her from the clutches of evil Cullen. Gil hopes his employment will improve his chances with Sally, but she eventually settles her affections on Peter Love. On the rebound, Gil edges toward Julia, who is more receptive to his advances.

The handsome Mark Singleton implores Stacey to give him a second chance with her, but Jamie Frame warns him to stay out of Stacey's life. The triangle acquires a fourth side when Mark's former wife Janet urges him to resume his run for the Senate. Danger soon adds further complication to the situation: Mark's newspaper campaign to expose political corruption has been almost too successful, and hired killers are now on his trail. Although Mark is back with Stacey now, he urges her, for her safety's sake, to pretend to be in love with Jamie. Unfortunately, the charade turns into reality. This despite the fact that Nicole is also in love with Jamie. But her cocaine problem prevents him from getting involved with her.

Mark encourages Stacey to feign love for Jamie to protect herself. His plan backfires, though, when Stacy really does fall for Jamie.

Best-selling writer Felicia Gallant falls for Cass Winthrop when he tries to lure her into his stable of writers.

Authoress Felicia has fallen for young publisher Cass, who is smitten with conniving Cecile. Cecile encourages Cass to get Felicia even further under his spell. Meanwhile a cassette arrives for Cecile from her former blackmailer, the awful Alma Rudder. Alma swears

Cecile is plotting again. This time it's Cass who's under her spell.

revenge on Sandy, a guy who isn't high on Cecile's list of favorite people, either. Alma disguises herself, calls herself "Nell" and gets a job waitressing at Smiley's Diner, where she spies on Sandy and Blaine. Murderous Alma tampers with the brakes in Sandy's car; the ensuing accident leaves him and Blaine unharmed. Finally, Alma hides in Sandy's prospective house and shoots him in the chest. Sandy hovers near death, while Larry, Julia, Gil, and Cass track down Alma. Her dead body is discovered, and Cecile (who has the murder weapon) is arrested and charged with the crime. She claims Alma was dead when she arrived at the scene, and it soon turns out she's telling the truth. It was Larry's mother Jeanne who accidentally caused Alma's death. Alma had attacked her with a knife and during the struggle fell on it. Cecile, not realizing she's been exonerated, drives through a storm and barely avoids going off a collapsed bridge.

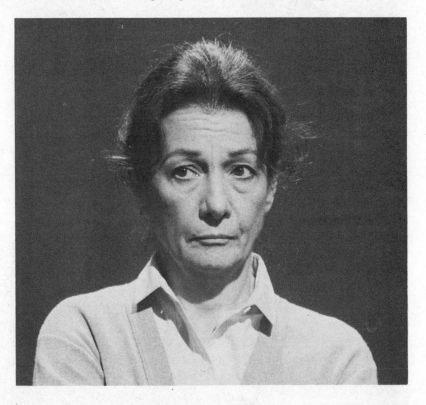

Jeanne accidentally caused Alma's death, but everyone is glad to see that awful woman buried.

The double marriage—Mac and Rachel, Sandy and Blaine—takes place amid great fanfare. Julia and Felicia make amends; after all, Rachel is not spiteful, but she *had* felt resentment when Julia, her assistant, published a bestselling book. Nicole is encouraged to return to modeling, but there are those (like Ted Bancroft and other drug suppliers) who would like to keep her addicted to her drug habit. She eventually accepts a modeling job for Felicia's new diet book. Blaine discovers she is pregnant, and her new husband Sandy is delighted.

Sally becomes engaged to Peter, whose sister Donna has been doing some checking and has learned that Sally once had a child

The double marriage of Mac to Rachel and Sandy to Blaine is a big event in Bay City.

These are happy times for Sandy and Blaine. She's found out she's pregnant, and they are both walking on air.

and gave him up for adoption. After her bridal shower, Sally is introduced to Jennifer Thatcher and young Kevin. Donna later reveals to Sally that Kevin is really Sally's son, the one she'd given up. Distressed, Sally postpones the wedding. Eventually, Sally meets Jennifer Thatcher's husband, David. Stunned, she recognizes him as the father of the child she gave away. And she realizes he must have told his wife the truth.

Felicia is jealous that Julia has written a bestseller, and she makes sure to pan Julia's second book. Felicia tells Cass she wants to be involved with editorial decision-making at Winthrop Publishing—including decisions regarding Julia.

Finally, the hired killers catch up with Mark Singleton. He pushes Janet to safety, but is himself shot and seriously wounded in the stomach. Stacey, who once loved him but now loves Jamie, hovers guiltily at Mark's bedside. Soon she realizes she is pregnant by Mark, and in her emotional confusion she ends up marrying him despite her love for Jamie.

Donna continues her efforts to keep Sally from marrying Peter, and goes so far as to warn David that she'll tell everybody about David and Sally's long ago love affair (and resultant love-child, Kevin) if the wedding takes place. Jennifer, Kevin's adoptive mother, is aghast when she overhears David and Sally discussing Kevin's real parentage. Jennifer takes the child and runs away, leaving a note saying that she'll never give the boy up. She leaves the child with friends of hers, and in her distraught state she is killed in a car crash. Sally comforts the boy, who blames his father for what has happened.

Sally can't comfort Peter, however, after she confesses to him that she'd once had an affair with David and that Kevin is in fact her son. Cecile is right there in a flash ready to offer Peter her sympathy.

Abel, meanwhile, is upset to see his twin, Leo, making advances to Quinn. Quinn, in turn, is intrigued by the new D.A. in town, Adam Banks, who mistakenly books Lily on charges of prostitution. He soon drops the charges.

Nicole is finding it impossible to drop her cocaine habit, and Felicia does what she can to get the girl professional help while Jamie sets out to prove that Ted is her drug supplier. It's not that Nicole hasn't tried. In fact, in early December we see her throw her cocaine to the winds. But Ted plants some more in her make-up case. Later he also plants some in Jamie's coat pocket, then calls the police. Jamie is arrested for possession; Stacey visits him in jail and offers to be his attorney.

David Thatcher proposes a business deal to Cass that's really a low-down scam. The idea is to make short-term windfall profits from companies that Mac Cory will buy. Cecile is recruited to dig up inside information on these companies, in ways that would not be approved of by John Houseman or the Federal Trade Commission. It is a storyline that will quickly turn dark and deep and carry over into 1984.

Profiles

Terry Davis
(Stacey Winthrop)

Terry Davis was born July 23, 1951, and raised in New York City. After picking up her B.A. degree in psychology at the College of New Rochelle, she played April Scott for four and a half years on *Edge of Night*. Terry is married to Andrew Weyman, her first soap opera director, and has a daughter, Sarah. She has also ventured into live theater, playing Lily in an off-Broadway production of *Toys in the Attic* and Cherie in a regional production of *Bus Stop*. She's been with *AW* since the fall of 1982.

Nancy Frangione
(Cecile dePoulignac)

Nancy Frangione vamps up a storm as the deliciously despicable Cecile on *AW*, a part she's played since summer 1981. She was born in Cape Cod, the fourth of eight children, studied acting with Uta Hagen, and got her big break (and her Equity card) when she played the character Jill in the Broadway production of *Equus*. Shortly thereafter, she landed the role of Tara on *All My Children* (1977–1979). She's done a number of off-off-Broadway roles since then, and is married to *AW* costar Chris Rich (Sandy Cory).

Laura Malone
(Blaine Cory)

Born in Seattle, Washington, Laura Malone attended the University of Washington, then found employment making commercials and playing in summer stock theatricals. Her next career move brought her to the Washington State Department of Justice where she made police training films. In July 1978 she undertook the role of Blaine on *AW* and in August 1982 married her longtime boyfriend, Val Gabriel. An avid sports fan, Laura collects and refinishes antique furniture, collects books, and enjoys playing Scrabble.

Petronia Paley
(Quinn Harding)

Born in Albany, Georgia, Petronia Paley graduated from Howard University, trained with the Negro Ensemble Company Acting Workshop and the New York Shakespeare Festival, and appeared on Broadway as Hope in *The First Breeze of Summer*. Before coming to *AW* in November 1981, Petronia played the role of Harriet Johnson in *One Life* and Dr. Jesse Rawlings in *The Doctors*. She recently starred in a PBS American Playhouse production, *Solomon Northrope's Odyssey*, directed by Gordon Parks, a film which will also have a theatrical release. A sensitive, even mystical, person, Petronia believes in reincarnation and practices Hatha Yoga.

Christopher Rich
(Sandy Cory)

The young Texas-born actor attended Pan American University and earned his Bachelor of Fine Arts degree from the University of Texas before going on to Cornell for his master's degree. He began his career as the lead in *Romeo and Juliet* at the Guthrie Theater in Minneapolis. Soon afterwards, he appeared in the Broadway production of *The Bacchae*, starring Irene Pappas. That's range— Dionysus to Sandy Cory—and in between these extremes, he's portrayed George in *Of Mice and Men*, and Christian in *Cyrano de Bergerac*. In 1981 he joined *AW* and the following year married *AW* costar Nancy Frangione.

Stephen Schnetzer
(Cass Winthrop)

One of ten finalists for the American College Theater Festival, Boston-raised Stephen Schnetzer was invited to audition for the New York Shakespeare Festival production of *Timon of Athens*. Soon he'd moved on to the company's *Cymbeline*, and from there to the Broadway production of *Talent for Murder*, with Claudette Colbert. The darkly handsome young actor also toured with Sir Michael Redgrave in *Shakespeare's People*. Then came television, including two years as Marcello Salta on *One Life* and a year and a half as Stephen Olsen on *Days of Our Lives*. He joined *AW* in mid-1982, shortly after marrying actress Nancy Snyder.

Douglass Watson
(Mackenzie Cory)

The silver-haired, Georgia-born actor began his career with Katharine Cornell in two Broadway plays, *Antony and Cleopatra* and *That Lady*. Since then he's appeared in over thirty Broadway productions, including Eugene O'Neill's *The Iceman Cometh*, for which he was reportedly hand-picked by the author. Indeed, Douglass Watson has been singled out for honors all his life, from the two Purple Hearts and Distinguished Flying Cross he won in World War II to the two Emmy Awards he received in 1979 and 1980. He joined the cast of *AW* in 1974.

Victoria Wyndham
(Rachel Davis)

Before coming to *Another World* in July 1972, Victoria Wyndham appeared for three years on *Guiding Light*. Interestingly, both her father and mother had played in *Guiding Light* when it was a radio serial. Victoria has also appeared on Broadway in *Fiddler on the Roof* (Bette Midler was a fellow cast member) and off-Broadway in experimental productions. She lives in Westchester County, New York, with her two children.

Arrivals and Departures

Richard Bekins
(Jamie Frame)

Richard Bekins, perhaps the most memorable of the Jamies, left that role early in 1983 after three and a half years. In that time Bekins's Jamie managed to give up drugs, divorce Cecile, be reunited with his real father, and write a bestselling novel. The character became so popular that at one point Richard found himself working 267 episodes in a row. Yet Richard was really a novice when he came to *AW*. The California-born actor studied at the American Academy of Dramatic Art and performed with the Los Angeles Shakespeare Festival before coming to New York to act in off-Broadway productions (including *My Prince, My King* and *Young Bucks*); but all that added up to only a year of professional acting experience. After *AW*, they won't call him inexperienced any more.

Linda Dano
(Felicia Gallant)

Besides being a successful actress, Linda Dano runs a fashion consulting business that sells clothes to five daytime dramas and selects wardrobes for such clients as Susan Lucci, Billie Jean King, and Robin Strasser. She began her rise to fame as a model, then as a contract player for 20th-Century-Fox. Before coming to *AW* in January 1983, she had played roles on two other soaps: Cynthia Haines on *As the World Turns* and Gretel Cummings on *One Life to Live*. In December 1981, she married advertising executive Frank Attardi, and in their free time the couple remodels their eighteenth-century farmhouse in Connecticut.

Kim Morgan Greene
(Nicole Love)

Beginning July 5, 1983, Kim Greene took on the role of Nicole, a beautiful young model fighting a dependency on cocaine. Kim brings her own experience as a model to the role. She is also a singer and dancer/choreographer and was a cast member of the Broadway hit, *42nd Street*. Other theater credits include *The Roar of the Greasepaint, the Smell of the Crowd, Grease*, and *Pippin*. Before joining *AW*, she played briefly on *Search, All My Children*, and *One Life*.

Joe Morton
(Dr. Abel Marsh/Leo Mars)

It was Joe Morton's idea to play a double role on *AW*. The twins, Abel and Leo, are a sort of Abel/Cain pair, and both are vying for the affections of lovely Quinn Harding. Born in Manhattan, Morton spent his early years as an Army brat in Europe. He's had a distinguished career in the theater, having been nominated for a Tony Award and having won a Theater World Award for the role of Walter Lee Younger in *Raisin in the Sun*. Other Broadway credits include *Hair* and *Two Gentlemen of Verona*. He also played in the films *And Justice for All* and *Arthur*, and played in *Search for Tomorrow* before coming to *AW* in February 1983. A single parent, Joe lives in Manhattan with his daughter, Hopi Noel.

Jennifer Runyon
(Sally Frame)

Jennifer Runyon made a strong impression as Sally Frame for the two years she played the role (spring 1981 to spring 1983). The young actress was born in Chicago and appeared in stage productions of *Plaza Suite* and *The Music Man*. She also landed a role in the movie, *To All a Good Night*, before testing the soapy waters of daytime drama. Jennifer lives in New York City and is fond of horseback riding and roller skating.

Kyra Sedgwick
(Julia Shearer)

From January 1982 until June of 1983, eighteen-year-old Kyra Sedgwick played the rebellious teenager, Julia, on *AW*. During the school year she wasn't allowed to work more than three days a week on the soap, and she had to juggle chores of memorizing lines and doing homework. Immediately on leaving the show, Kyra made her off-Broadway debut as a high-schooler named Moxie in *Time Was*, at the St. Clements Theatre. She had to miss her own high school graduation as a result, but was able to make the class party after the show.

Robin Thomas
(Mark Singleton)

Pennsylvania-born Robin Thomas was a teenage science whiz kid who studied acting in college before switching to a career in sculpture. Since coming to Manhattan in 1972, his kinetic sculpture has been displayed in a number of galleries, even in the light-hearted "Edible Art" show in New York's SoHo section. For a while, Robin also had a contracting business; and his most famous clients were John Lennon and Yoko Ono, during their Dakota days. Robin returned to acting, appearing in the films *Prince of the City* and *Boys in the Band*, as well as in the TV movie, *Svengali*, with Peter O'Toole. He joined the cast of *AW* in March 1983.

Stephen Yates
(Jamie Frame)

When Jamie appeared unexpectedly at the double wedding on August 4, many viewers must have done a double take. Jamie somehow looked different. In fact, a new actor, Stephen Yates, had taken over the role from the popular Richard Bekins, who had become a tough act to follow. But Stephen is no novice; he played artist Ben McFarren on *Guiding Light* for four years and before that (in 1977) had played Chris Pierson for six months on *AW*. Raised in Illinois, Stephen graduated from Northwestern before moving to San Francisco, where he worked with the American Conservatory Theatre. Besides acting, he's expert at sailing and regards his twenty-one-day transatlantic sail from the Grand Canary Islands to Barbados as one of the most fulfilling experiences of his life. Bay City should pose no problems after that!

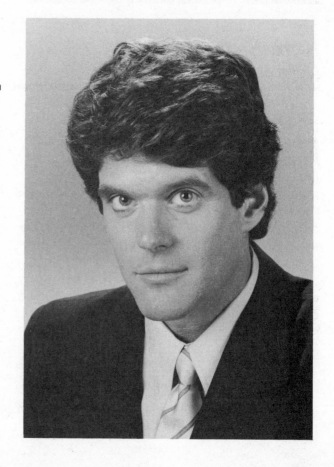

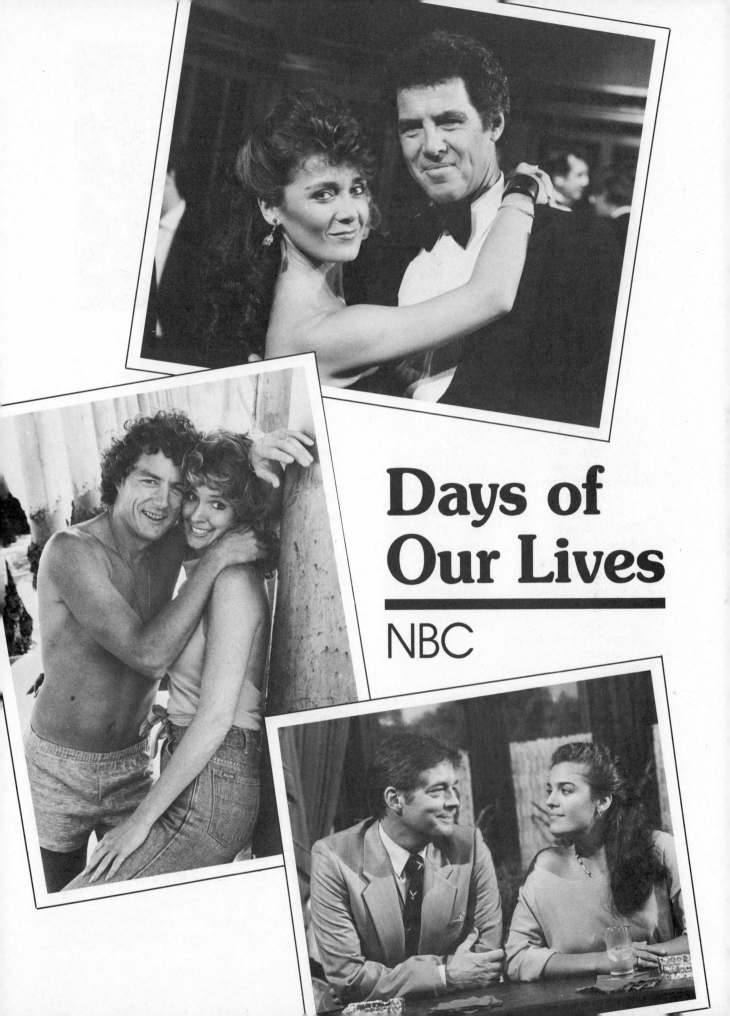

Days of
Our Lives

NBC

The Cast

Kristian Alfonso (new in
  spring)................. Hope Williams
Jed Allan................. Don Craig
Andrea Barber........... Carrie Brady
Richard Bergman
  (joined in late
  summer).............. Brett Fredricks
Dick Billingsley.......... Scotty Banning
Roger Aaron Brown..... Danny Grant
Ruth Buzzi (guest
  appearances)........ Leticia
Macdonald Carey...... Tom Horton
Lane Caudell............ Woody King
John Clarke.............. Mickey Horton
Robert Clary (left early
  in year)................ Robert LeClair
Barbara Crampton (left
  in October)........... Trista Evans
Marty Davich............ Marty the pianist
Shirley de Burgh........ Delia Abernathy
John deLancie.......... Eugene Bradford
Don Frabotta............ Dave the waiter
Joe Gallison............. Dr. Neil Curtis
Deidre Hall.............. Dr. Marlena Evans-
                         Brady
Bill Hayes................ Doug Williams
Susan Seaforth
  Hayes................. Julie Williams
Leann Hunley............ Anna Brady-DiMera
Kathleen King (left in
  spring)................ Gretchen
Michael Leon (started in
  fall).................... Pete Jennings
Gloria Loring........... Liz Chandler

Debbie Lytton (left early
  in year)............... Melissa Anderson
Anne-Marie Martin...... Gwen Davies
Gregg Marx............. David Banning
Joseph Mascolo (left in
  spring)................ Stefano DiMera
Wayne Northrop........ Roman Brady
Thaao Penghlis......... Antony DiMera
Peter Reckell (new in
  spring)................ Bo Brady
Quinn Redeker.......... Alex Marshall
Frances Reid............ Alice Horton
James Reynolds........ Abe Carver
Madlyn Rhue (started in
  spring)................ Daphne DiMera
Suzanne Rogers........ Maggie Horton
Pamela Roylance
  (started in
  summer).............. Sandy Horton
Philece Sampler (left in
  summer).............. Renee Banning
Lanna Saunders........ Marie Curtis
Jean Bruce Scott (left
  early in year)........ Jessica Horton
Shawn Stevens.......... Oliver Martin
Catherine Mary
  Stewart............... Kayla Brady
Josh Taylor.............. Chris Kositchek
Lisa Trusel (started in
  spring)................ Melissa Anderson
Donna Wilkes (left in
  summer).............. Pamela

Executive
producers: Mrs. Ted Corday, Al Rabin
Producers: Ken Corday, Patricia Wenig
Directors: Joe Behar, Kenn Herman, Susan
           Simon
Head writer: Margaret DePriest
Writers: Sheri Anderson, Maralyn
         Thoma, Steven J. Fisher

Background

Days of Our Lives completed eighteen years on the air November 8, 1983, and still boasts several original cast members: Macdonald Carey as Dr. Tom Horton, Frances Reid as his wife Alice, and John Clarke in the role of their son, Mickey Horton. Around these "tentpole" characters cluster a number of friends, relatives, and enemies, all living out the days of their lives in the fictional town of Salem, U.S.A.— that is, when they're not battling cobras in the jungles outside Caracas or pursuing the mystery of the "Bradford Curse" in Haiti.

In fact, the show has become a study in juxtaposition between the domestic and the outlandish. Psychic premonitions, death-dealing robots, serial murders with voodoo overtones seem to alternate with common domestic quarrels and jealousies, as if Dr. Who and Dr. No found themselves trapped in a house where father knows best.

Nineteen eighty-three was the year when psychiatrist Dr. Marlena Evans married handsome Roman Brady, despite assassination attempts against him. It was the year when mob kingpin Stefano DiMera caused numerous deaths until he was finally apprehended. It was a year jingling with romantic triangles, Liz and Marie cat-fighting for Neil's affections, and Don and Maggie falling in love while Mag's husband Mickey is away being bitten by snakes. An exhaustingly entertaining year, in fact, which makes one wonder: What more can they possibly do in 1984?

The Story

The word around Salem is that anybody who has anything to do with Roman is in danger, now that he's after mob boss Stefano. Roman's sister Kayla is almost killed and, while she's in the hospital recovering, Stefano's henchman Alex sends the robot to poison her. Kayla slips into a coma, but recovers.

Alex helps his boss pick the next victim: Alice Horton. Gretchen hears Alex talking about this, and Chris spots him tinkering with the robot. Before long, Gretchen is poisoned by the potion meant for Alice. Dying, she's just able to tell Doug that she heard someone plotting to kill Alice.

Mickey's in trouble, too. On the run from Stefano's men in the jungle, he's bitten by a snake. Delirious, Mickey is recaptured and dragged back to his jungle prison. It will be late March before he makes his escape.

By that time, a lot has happened in Salem. Liz tries to get evidence that her husband, Tony DiMera, has been fooling around with Renee. Liz is frightened of the DiMeras and wants to be free to go after Neil (by whom she has become pregnant), although Neil has grown deeply attached to Marie. Liz and Marie detest each other as a result. Don also has romantic problems: he's falling in love with Mickey's wife, Maggie. Eventually, she returns his love. When Mickey gets back to Salem at last he overhears Don and Maggie admitting their love for each other and falls down, stricken with a heart attack.

Finally, Roman and Marlena decide the time has come to get married. Alex plots an ambush for Roman, planting a hit man in the tuxedo store. Roman recognizes the man's face from a mug shot and after a desperate struggle the thug's gun goes off. Abe and Don rush in to find Roman unconscious and the goon dead. At the church, yet another assassination attempt delays the wedding, but finally Roman and Marlena are married. Afterwards, the new bride goes off on the "honeymoon" while Roman goes underground to investigate Stefano. He succeeds in getting evidence about Stefano's criminal activities, but then discovers that Liz and Marlena have disappeared. A desperate Stefano is holding them while he

Roman and Marlena's happiness is continually threatened by his investigation of mob boss Stefano. They are finally married, in spite of two attempts to rub out Roman.

The provisions of Stefano's will have bizarre consequences for Renee and Tony. In order to inherit his millions, they must live under the same roof, even though they are now married to other people.

waits for a getaway helicopter at his mountain hideout. Liz goes into labor, has the baby, and slips into unconsciousness before she can tell Neil that he's the father of the child. Stefano is captured and hauled off to jail, where he dies of a stroke after a heartrending farewell to his daughter Renee.

Sensitive Eugene finally begins to get close to reluctant Trista, who nonetheless keeps from him secrets about her background. She has also suppressed most memories of her mother's murder. When Oliver finds Pamela passed out from drugs, Marlena vows to start a youth crisis center.

Tony and Renee are stunned by the provisions in Stefano's will. Back in 1982, it will be remembered, Tony and Renee had fallen in love, not realizing they were siblings. Then they found out and had to break up (incest being something even the DiMeras frown upon). Stefano's will tries to bring the family together by stipulating that Tony and Renee have to live under the same roof for a year in order to inherit the DiMera millions. Also, Renee must remain married to David, whom she latched onto on the rebound from Tony, whom she still loves.

Apparently, Stefano's will was written before it was learned that Renee and Tony were *not* brother and sister after all. Now that they're both married to other people, how could they possibly live together in the same house? David and Tony both reject the will's provisions, but their wives seem willing to do almost anything to get their hands on the money.

Eventually, a second will is found, leaving the money to Renee with no stipulations. Unfortunately, she never gets her hands on it, since she's murdered toward the end of summer.

Using her own key, Liz lets herself into Neil's home and waits in his bed for him to show up. She's determined to win him away from Marie. A storm is raging outside as Neil enters. He's furious to find Liz there but lust soon takes over. They make love but then he's called away to the hospital on an emergency. Left alone, Liz hears a crash of glass and goes downstairs, gun in hand. Hands trembling, she fires at the "prowler," only to find the slumped form is her arch-rival Marie. Liz calls the paramedics but, fearful about what she's done, flees the scene. Eventually, Marie recovers from her wounds. Neil falls deeply in love with Liz. By accident, the two meet up with each other at the same vacation resort and are unable to keep their hands off each other. Soon, though, Liz is tried and convicted for attempted murder, and is sentenced to five years in prison.

The struggle for the DiMera money continues, and Renee rigs a boat to sink and kill Anna. Unfortunately, Tony is also in the boat and is knocked unconscious when it sinks. David happens by and saves both Tony and Anna, who eventually loses her baby.

Meanwhile Trista is definitely being followed; attempts are made to steal her old letters and other personal material. Bo continues to investigate the murder of Barbara Talmadge (Trista's mother), and Eugene and Trista continue to become more involved with each other. Trista is finally able to remember a long-suppressed image: the place where she hid the gun her mother was killed by. As she takes it from inside the grandfather clock, Alex Marshall suddenly appears and snatches it from her. Bo arrives and overpowers the cad; and then good old Eugene shows up, dragging with him a lost lover of Alex's, a woman named Nora. She's the one, it eventuates, who killed Trista's Mom. The motive: jealousy.

Eugene and Trista are in love; but there's a problem, a thing called "the Bradford curse." Gene's grandfather in Haiti has just died and the curse now hangs around Gene's shoulders. In fact, people suddenly do start dropping like flies.

Feeling rejected by Tony, Renee (now divorced from David) marries Alex, only afterwards realizing that Stefano's second will leaves everything to her without strings. It homes in on her that Alex knew this and married her for her money. She schemes to expose his chicanery at a big party at the DiMera mansion. Dressed to kill or be killed, she sweeps down the stairs and makes the dramatic announcement that her new husband is a louse who will never touch her again. Then she lashes out at her enemies, one by one: Doug, Julie, David, Anna, Alex, Daphne, and the whole Horton family. She loves only one person: Tony, even though he has rejected her.

On the rebound from Tony, Renee marries Alex, but later realizes he was only after her money.

Gwen, Terry, and Sandy enjoy themselves at Renee's bash; at least until Renee lashes out at the entire Horton family.

Renee may have been found with a knife in her back, but Philece Sampler, the actress who played the part, had a much nicer send-off.

Tony is so impressed by Renee's spunk that he gives her white roses and confesses he's always loved her. They make love upstairs while the party continues. In the stables, meanwhile, Gene proposes to Trista. As their lips meet, the sound of a scream comes from the house. Delia rushes into the livingroom crying out, "Murder!" Renee has just been found with a knife in her back. Clutched in her hand: a black feather.

The mystery deepens when it turns out that the real cause of death was poisoning. Soon after, Kelly is found dead, and Gene vows to solve the string of murders by going to Haiti. While there he and Trista have a romantic wedding; but their joy is short-lived. In fact, Trista is short-lived. She's found murdered, and in her hand a raven's feather. Back in Salem, Gwen is attacked but escapes unharmed. Sought for questioning by the police, Eugene is hidden by his eccentric cousin Leticia, who is herself quickly dispatched by the mysterious murderer. Eugene is taken into custody.

Roman becomes obsessed with solving the serial murders, and gradually he and Marlena begin to drift apart. Then it appears that Liz is marked for murder. Finally, Sandy and Marlena think they catch a glimpse of the murderer in the act of killing Daisy. It appears to be

Roman! Reluctantly, Abe arrests him. Roman insists that he is being framed, and Marlena sides with him, refusing to believe the mounting evidence against him.

Liz and Neil have been planning a prison wedding, not realizing that several inmates are planning their escape that day. In fact, their marriage plans are knocked into a cocked hat when Liz is shot during the prison break. She recovers eventually, but finds herself with a serious amnesia problem. Yes, the Asian flu of the soap world has struck her down, leaving her so confused she thinks she's married to Don.

Roman, meanwhile, has made good his own escape from jail, and a shaken Alice Horton is arrested for helping him do it. Roman feels he must be on the outside looking for evidence that will clear him. Anna, as it happens, is running for her life from Salem (Alex is after her). By chance, she ends up with Roman, and the two of them throw in their lot together, two fugitives on the run.

The year ends on a happier note, however. At the end of December there's a great big birthday party for Hope, who has just turned eighteen.

Anna is on the run from Salem and Alex, and eventually runs into Roman, also on the lam.

Profiles

Jed Allan
(Don Craig)

Born in the Bronx, New York, Jed Allan went a long way—to the famous Pasadena Playhouse—to study acting; then he came back to New York to drive cabs while waiting for some sort of break in his acting career. TV came to his rescue, with a six-month stint on *Love of Life*, a one-year role on *Secret Storm*, and thirty episodes of *Lassie*. Jed has also hosted TV's *Celebrity Bowling* and various game shows and was featured in the TV movie, *Real Friends*. He took on the role of Don on *DOOL* in 1975.

Macdonald Carey
(Dr. Tom Horton)

Macdonald Carey, who has been playing doctor roles since the 1940s, when he portrayed a medic on NBC radio, is one of the original cast members of *DOOL*. Since 1965, he's been honored with two Emmy Awards for his characterization of Tom Horton and was recently cited by the Television Academy of Arts and Sciences for his forty years' achievement as a performer. The Iowa-born actor's first break was a big one: starring on Broadway in 1939 opposite Gertrude Lawrence in *Lady In the Dark*. Since then, he's done other plays and over fifty motion pictures, ranging from *Gidget Gets Married* to *American Gigolo*. Mr. Carey has six grown children and lives in Beverly Hills.

Joe Gallison
(Dr. Neil Curtis)

Two decades on TV soaps and the man still appears to be sane. Joe Gallison reportedly appeared in over a thousand episodes of *Another World* before going on to *One Life to Live* and *Return to Peyton Place*. Born in Boston, Joe was a math major at Northeastern University before plunging into acting. Under contract to Warner Brothers, he played in *PT-109*, *Critic's Choice*, and other movies before succumbing to the blandishments of daytime drama. He joined *DOOL* in 1974.

Deidre Hall
(Dr. Marlena Evans-Brady)

Vivacious Deidre Hall is one of soaplands most visible and popular stars. She was raised in Florida, where she hosted her own radio program on WLIZ and disc-jockeyed on WQXT. Before coming to *DOOL* in June 1976, Deidre had a recurring role for three years on *The Young and the Restless*. She has also made appearances on *The Tonight Show*, *Columbo*, *Night Gallery* and others, and is a regular guest on game shows.

Bill Hayes
(Doug Williams)

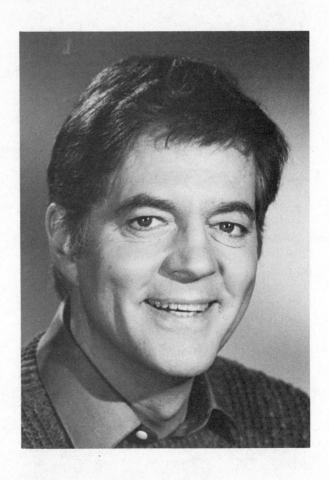

It's been a varied (not to say checkered) career for Chicago-born Bill Hayes. Long before joining *DOOL* in 1970, Bill was a featured singer on Sid Caesar's legendary *Your Show of Shows*. He went on to earn a gold record for his rendition of "The Ballad of Davy Crockett." It makes a nice contrast on the shelf next to his master's degree from Northwestern University. In 1974, he married *DOOL* costar Susan Seaforth and the following year was nominated for an Emmy as best daytime actor. The couple lives in North Hollywood, California.

Susan Seaforth Hayes
(Julie Williams)

Since making her debut at the age of four with the Metropolitan Opera Company, Susan Seaforth Hayes has reportedly appeared in some two hundred films, TV shows, and stage productions. She starred as Ado Annie in the touring company of *Oklahoma!*, among many other roles, but seems to have found a satisfying niche in daytime TV, joining *DOOL* in 1968. She and her husband, fellow *DOOL* star Bill Hayes, are always involved in some project and recently opened their own soap opera workshop in Hollywood. The final class of the course was an actual taping of a half-hour student-produced soap. The diploma: a videotape of the edited results—suitable for use in soap auditions.

Leann Hunley
(Anna Brady-DiMera)

The youngest of four children, Leann attended the University of Washington but impulsively quit shortly before graduation in order to move to Hawaii. It was there she landed her first TV role, in *Hawaii Five-O*. She brings some of that same impulsiveness, not to say impetuousness, to the role of Anna, which she undertook in 1982. She's also been seen in the theatrical films *Xanadu* and *Buck Rogers in the 25th Century*. Her vampishly glamorous looks have landed her in numerous TV commercials and have not hurt in getting her roles in *Fantasy Island*, *The Islander*, *Battlestar: Galactica*, *BJ and the Bear*, and other TV shows.

Gloria Loring
(Liz Chandler)

Married to Canadian talk show host Alan Thicke, Gloria Loring is extremely well-known as a singer, and is said to have made more than three hundred TV appearances in that capacity on such programs as *The Tonight Show*, *The Carol Burnett Show*, and *The Glenn Campbell Show*. She also regularly sings the National Anthem at Los Angeles Dodgers games. A central character on *DOOL* since 1980, Gloria is also a woman of many projects. She wrote the theme song for NBC's *The Facts of Life* and compiled the *Days of Our Lives Celebrity Cookbook*, through which she raised half a million dollars for the Juvenile Diabetes Foundation.

Wayne Northrop
(Roman Brady)

A driving force on *DOOL* since he joined the show in 1981, Wayne Northrop has brought his special intensity to a variety of roles, including Ralph Waite's award-winning stage production of *The Kitchen*. Born in a small town in Washington State, the actor graduated from the University of Washington and then spent nearly two years working at odd jobs in Europe. Since discovering television some years back, Wayne has appeared on *Police Story*, *Baretta*, *Eight Is Enough*, and *The Waltons*. In 1980 he played the chauffeur, Michael, on *Dynasty*.

Suzanne Rogers
(Maggie Horton)

If you had a sharp eye, you might have picked Suzanne out of the line of Rockettes at Radio City Music Hall a few years back. The former chorus girl was soon appearing in Broadway productions of *110 in the Shade*, *Funny Girl*, *Hallelujah, Baby!*, *Coco*, and *Follies*. It's not surprising that she began her career as a dancer, back in her home town of Colonial Heights, Virginia. Since joining the cast of *DOOL* she won the 1979 Emmy for outstanding supporting actress in a soap.

Arrivals and Departures

Kristian Alfonso
(Hope Williams)

Born in Brockton, Massachusetts, young Kristian Alfonso was always interested in dance and figure skating and in 1978 won the Junior Olympic figure skating championship. She began pursuing a modeling career while still in high school and after graduating began taking acting classes. Kristian made several TV commercials and landed a part in the NBC miniseries *The Star Maker* before joining *DOOL* in spring of 1983.

Joseph Mascolo
(Stefano DiMera)

In a short time, Joe Mascolo made himself one of the great daytime Iagos, a mob chieftain who loves his family and has no regard for human life. He's good at this kind of role, having played a similar character in NBC's *The Gangster Chronicles*. In his earlier days, the musically gifted actor was offered a Fulbright scholarship to conduct opera, and recently he sang a duet with Luciano Pavarotti. He also used to play clarinet with the Metropolitan Opera Orchestra. He appeared on Broadway and in London in *That Championship Season* and in Arthur Miller's *A View from the Bridge*, and he performs regularly at Burt Reynolds's dinner theater in Jupiter, Florida. He left *DOOL* in the spring of 1983.

Peter Reckell
(Bo Brady)

Joining *DOOL* in spring 1983, Peter Reckell was already familiar with the machinations of daytime storylines, having played on *As the World Turns*. Born in Lansing, Michigan, he moved with his family to Indiana when he was three and later attended the Boston Conservatory of Music, majoring in theater, voice, and music. He also traveled with a theater group for a while, getting dust on his shoes and credits on his resume. In his free time Peter enjoys singing, dancing, and carpentry.

Philece Sampler
(Renee Banning)

Before coming to *DOOL* in the major role of Renee, Philece Sampler had done a bit of television, including segments of *BJ and the Bear* and *Fantasy Island*, as well as the movie *Phantom of the Paradise*. The young Texas-born actress had also trod the boards in dinner theater productions of *Charley's Aunt* and *Under the Yum Yum Tree*, and had toured in *The Latest Mrs. Adam* and *My Three Angels*. She lives in the Lake Hollywood section of Los Angeles.

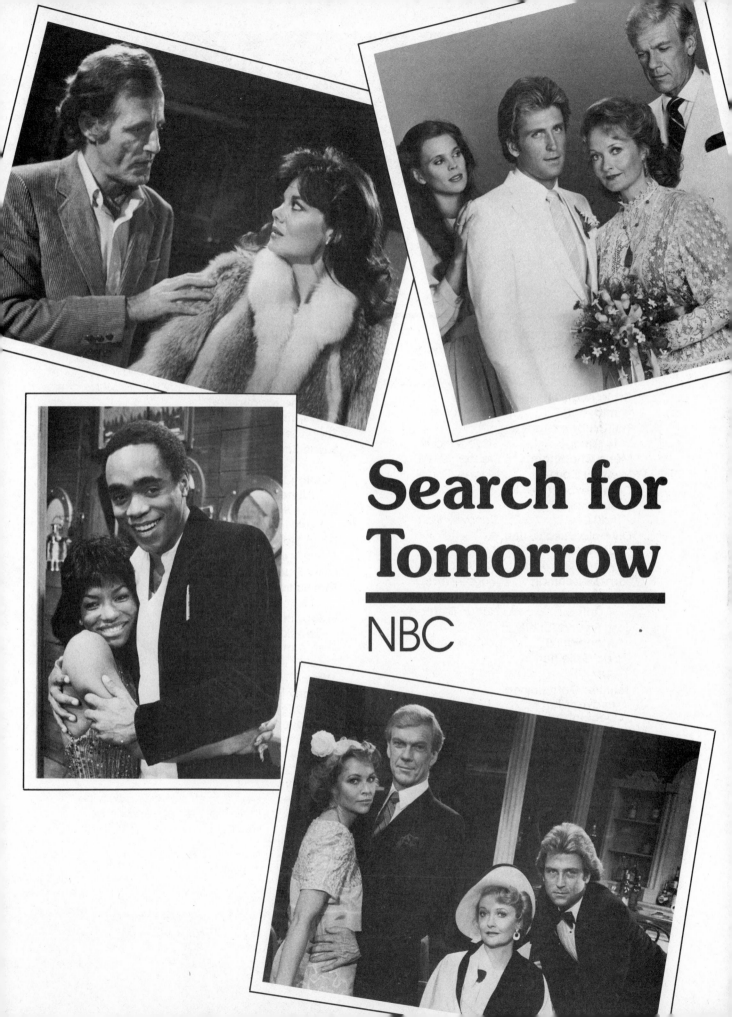

Search for Tomorrow
NBC

The Cast

Jay Acavone (started in March) .... *Brian Emerson*
John Aniston .... *Martin Tourneur*
Rod Arrants .... *Travis Tourneur Sentell*
Craig Augustine (left midyear) .... *Keith McNeil*
Philip Brown (started in spring) .... *Steve Kendall*
Marie Cheatham ..... *Stephanie Wyatt*
Michael Corbett ...... *Warren Carter*
Cain DeVore (new in summer, left late fall) .... *Danny Walton*
Olympia Dukakis (left at end of year) .... *Barbara Moreno*
Larry Fleischman ...... *Ringo Altman*
David Forsyth (joined in fall) .... *Hogan McLeary*
Josh Freund (briefly in spring only) .... *Josh Moreno*
David Gale (left in spring) .... *Rusty Sentell*
Jennifer Gatti (joined midyear, left in December) .... *Angela Moreno*
Cynthia Gibb (left in summer) .... *Suzi Wyatt Carter*
Linda Gibboney (left end of summer) .... *Jenny Deacon*
Stacey Glick .... *Andy McNeil*
John Glover (left end of November) ...... *Vargas*
Larry Haines .... *Stu Bergman*
Peter Haskell (new midyear) .... *Lloyd Kendall*
Tina Johnson (new in spring) .... *Rhonda Sue Huckaby*
Mitch Litrofsky (left early in year) .... *Tom Bergman*

Robert LuPone (began early in year) .... *Tom Bergman*
Sherry Mathis .... *Liza Sentell*
Marcia McCabe ...... *Sunny Adamson*
Susan Monts .... *Prof. Aja Doyan*
Lisa Peluso .... *Wendy Wilkins McNeil*
Gene Pietragallo (left in spring) .... *Brian Emerson*
Sheryl Lee Ralph ...... *Mac*
Susan Scannell .... *Kristin Carter Emerson*
Damion Scheller (new in June) .... *Josh Moreno*
Marcus Smythe (left early in year) .... *Dane Taylor*
Doug Stevenson (left early in year) .... *Lee Sentell*
Mary Stuart .... *Joanne Tourneur*
Tom Sullivan (left end of summer) .... *Michael Kendall*
Elizabeth Swackhamer (new in summer, left in fall) .... *Suzi Wyatt Carter*
Wayne Tippit (left early in year) .... *Ted Adamson*
Tom Wright (left midyear) .... *John Carver Colton, Jr.*

Executive producer: *Ellen Barrett (replacing Joanna Lee, who left near end of the year)*
Supervising producer: *H. Ted Busch*
Producer: *Robert Getz*
Associate producers: *Gail Starkey, Bonnie S. Bogard*
Directors: *Ned Stark, Robert Schwarz*
Writers: *Gary Tomlin, Jeanne Glynn, Leslie Thomas*

Background

"Mary and I were doing a Kraft Theater," recalls Anna Lee, who plays the silver-haired matriarch, Lila Quartermaine, on *General Hospital*; "and she said, 'Well, I've got to go for an interview this afternoon for a soap opera. . . . You know, it'll probably only run several weeks and I'll be back.'"

Thus did young Mary Stuart start her role as Joanne "Jo" Tourneur on *Search for Tomorrow* in September 1951. So completely has Jo turned into a fixture of our popular culture that many fans tell Miss Stuart, "I've known you all my life." One man in Seattle particularly delighted her recently. "He said, 'Chicken soup. I just look at you and I can smell chicken soup, because I had that every day for lunch when I came home from school.'"

As the only original cast member still with the show, Miss Stuart has seen many changes, from the rudimentary staging of the fifties, when a windowframe was hung in front of a black curtain to indicate a wall, to the freewheeling sixties, when Jill Clayburgh, Susan Sarandon, Don Knotts, Lee Grant, Roy Scheider, and others were on the show, to the "frantic, back-to-the-kids stuff" that started in the late seventies and still pertains today.

The year 1983 will be memorable for Mary Stuart because for the first time in about seven years she was given a juicy storyline: Jo's kidnapping by the psychopathic Vargas (played by John Glover). Before that, "It was this-way-to-your-table for quite a long time," she admits.

The front-burner drama for the last couple of years has centered on the lives of Liza and Travis Sentell (played by Sherry Mathis and Rod Arrants), their friends and family in the fictional town of Henderson. In 1983, a very hot triangle develops involving Warren Carter (played by Michael Corbett), teenager Wendy McNeil (Lisa Peluso), and Wendy's best friend, Suzi (Cindy Gibb and then Elizabeth Swackhamer), who happens to be Warren's wife. The evolution of Wendy over the past few years from innocent cutie-pie to full-fledged vamp undergoes an exciting acceleration during 1983.

Search is the longest-running television-originated daytime drama. After thirty years on the air, it made the switch from CBS to NBC in March of 1982. Competing for viewers with ABC's *Ryan's Hope* and CBS's *The Young and the Restless*, *Search*'s ratings have not been encouraging in recent years. Yet for old time's sake, and for the millions of fans who are devoted to Jo and Stu and Liza and Travis, one hopes that the show's search for ratings is rewarded with many more tomorrows.

The Story

Nasty Rusty Sentell, conniving Warren Carter, and psychopathic Vargas manage to raise a lot of hell during 1983. Rusty is particularly unrelenting in his efforts to break up his son Travis's marriage with Liza. The old gunrunner would rather have his goddaughter, Professor Aja Doyan, married to Travis. So would Aja, who's obsessed with Travis. She tries to stall him at the airport when he wants to fly to New York to surprise Liza, but he takes off anyway, only to find that Liza has left for Toronto. Rusty later makes sure that Travis finds out that Liza went out discoing while she was up there. When flowers mysteriously arrive for Liza, Travis accuses her of having an affair. Soon Liza finds out that she's pregnant, but worries that Travis will think the baby is not his.

Keith McNeil and Wendy secretly get married; when she finds out about it, Wendy's mother Stephanie demands that they have the marriage annulled. McNeil's diabetic twelve-year-old daughter, Andy, doesn't approve of the marriage either. She's given to acts of truancy, running away, and shoplifting. For a while Andy stays with Stephanie and makes existence a trial for her. At last she comes to accept her

Wendy and Keith marry in secret. They can't keep it quiet for long, though, and Wendy's mother is furious when she finds out about the wedding.

Twelve-year-old Andy has had a tough time of it, but her friendship with Josh will help ease the way.

diabetic condition and (even more important) the fact that Jenny is her real mother. Later, Andy and an equally young Josh Moreno establish a tentative friendship.

Eager police recruit Brian Emerson has always loved Suzi, but Kristin has managed to get pregnant by him. Out of conscience, he marries Kristin, not knowing that she has already miscarried. With Stephanie's connivance, Kristin later flies to Detroit to fake a miscarriage. When she calls to tell him the news, Brian is sad about the loss of the baby but elated to be free of his obligation to Kristin. He rushes to declare his love for Suzi, only to find that she is married to Warren Carter.

Suzi has married Warren Carter, and she's in for a lot of heartache.

Warren reluctantly accepts a gun-running job from Rusty, though it means he must deceive Suzi. That's not the only way he deceives her. He's soon involved in a torrid affair with Suzi's best friend, Wendy, who is beginning to wonder if her own hasty marriage to Keith might have been a mistake.

If you can't trust your best friend and your husband, whom can you trust? Poor Suzi is deceived by the two people closest to her.

And then, Rusty is found shot dead. To protect his wife, Travis confesses to the murder and manages to conceal evidence that could implicate Liza. Later Liza herself confesses, believing herself guilty. (She had fired two shots and didn't realize that both had missed.) Finally, Aja is confronted with Tom and Dane's conclusive evidence against her, and she confesses, explaining that Rusty had been manipulating too many people's lives. Finally, after a long separation, Liza invites her husband Travis to stay over. At about this time, Travis goes into therapy and discovers he has violently angry feelings toward his dead father, Rusty.

Jo discovers that Suzi's trust fund is worth four million dollars, but Tom doesn't think the girl should be told about it because her husband, Warren, can't be trusted. Wendy finds herself pregnant by Warren, and even worse, in love with him; and she convinces him to divorce Suzi and marry her. That's when Warren finds out about Suzi's trust fund. Divorce is suddenly out of the question. An abortion for Wendy is more to his liking.

Travis finds Rusty shot dead. To protect his wife, who he suspects committed the crime, he confesses to the murder.

Then, in late summer, a psychotic criminal named Vargas—a shady associate of Warren's—grabs Jo and kidnaps her. Shortly afterwards, Liza and Travis step into Stephanie's car and very nearly have a fatal accident. Warren is suspicious and accuses Vargas of tampering with the brakes; after all, Vargas had vowed to get even with Stephanie for giving Warren a hard time. (She had made some angry remark which crazy Vargas had misinterpreted.) Warren begins to realize how out of control Vargas is and soon begins to wonder if he might not be the one who abducted Jo.

Vargas, a psychotic criminal, holds Jo captive in an abandoned warehouse.

The madman alternately torments and attends to Jo, calling her his mother. In a desperate move, Jo starts a fire and makes a dash for freedom, but Vargas recaptures her. Meanwhile, her car is found in the river, along with her purse, and soon Jo is given up for dead. A memorial service is held for her, which Vargas secretly attends. When a trained psychic mentions that she doesn't feel that Jo is dead, Vargas follows the medium home and injects her with a chemical which induces a fatal heart attack.

Liza and Travis's baby arrives a bit earlier than scheduled, but he's healthy and they're happy.

Liza's baby is born premature but all right—the labor induced by the car accident—and she and Travis name him Tourneur Stuart Martin Sentell. Meanwhile, Jenny and Michael plan their own wedding.

Vargas informs Martin that Jo is still alive and that if he wants to see her again he'd better come up with $250,000 quick. Martin raises the cash and, packing a gun, goes to meet Vargas. Brian and Kristin are also hot on the trail, which leads to a seemingly abandoned warehouse. In the struggle which ensues, Martin is shot and Vargas is thrown through a window into the murky water below. Jo is rescued, angry, hungry, and traumatized.

After the traumatic events they've just been through, Brian and Kristin try to establish an honest basis for their marriage. Kristin confesses to him that she'd lost their baby before their wedding and had later faked a miscarriage once they were married. Brian is stunned by this news and decides to move out of their apartment for a while and think things through.

As Steve Kendall and Stephanie Wyatt make final preparations for their own wedding, Lloyd Kendall storms in and announces that he isn't really Steve's father; Martin Tourneur is. This fact is something

Lloyd's wife had confessed once in anger when Steve was eight years old. Upon learning this, Steve rushes to the wounded Martin's bedside.

Meanwhile, in Jo's hospital room where she's recovering from her ordeal, the shadowy figure of Vargas appears! Soon we see him stalking Suzi. Failing to find her, he murders Joy in Warren's apartment. Then he manages to grab Jo again and hold her captive. The madman is ultimately hunted down and killed by Brian and Steve.

Wendy has seduced Warren again and urges him to divorce Suzi, but he's determined not to discard Suzi until after her approaching birthday, when she inherits the millions Warren covets. Soon, though, Wendy loses Warren's baby. Though a thorough scoundrel, Warren is saddened by the loss. Then Brian shows up, incensed at Warren's treatment of Suzi (and everyone else), and punches the cad out.

Warren, after all, is no sweetheart. He had doctored the club's books to make it seem that Martin, not he himself, had been embezzling funds. And now he arranges for three million dollars' worth of diamonds to be planted in Martin's suitcase, so that Martin will not be cleared of the embezzlement charges.

What happens then confuses even Warren: The diamonds disappear. After Vargas's death, Jo recalls her captor having said that he had left several million dollars "under the rose." When that story appears in the paper, Warren is sure he's on the trail of the diamonds. And indeed, the missing diamonds had been secreted in a box with a rose printed on its cover. Hogan, Sunny, and Kristin, on the trail of the loot, break into Vargas's apartment to find the place completely done in roses—even the bedspread has a rose pattern!

Sunny and Hogan try to unravel the mystery left by the death of Vargas.

Sunny learns from a secret source about Vargas's connection with Warren, and other matters. But refusing to reveal her source, she ends up in jail for contempt of court.

Warren, meanwhile, at Wendy's urging, throws a big Christmas party for all the little kids Suzi has been working with.

Profiles

Rod Arrants
(Travis Tourneur Sentell)

Before joining *Search* in October 1978, Rod Arrants made his daytime debut in *The Young and the Restless*. He also portrayed Austin Cushing in NBC's *Lovers and Friends* and recreated the role in the serial drama, *For Richer, For Poorer*. Rod's own career seems to have been for better and better. He studied at the American Conservatory Theatre in San Francisco and later started his own theater. As teacher and artist-in-residence at Mills College (Oakland, California), he directed numerous productions. He is married to actress Patricia Estrin, who played the role of Dr. Jamie Larson on *Search* for part of 1980. The couple lives in Brooklyn Heights, New York, with their two sons, Dylan (born 1969) and Zachary (born 1971).

Marie Cheatham
(Stephanie Wyatt)

After originating the role of Marie on *Days of Our Lives*, Marie Cheatham came to *Search* in January 1974. Before that, the blonde, green-eyed Oklahoman worked in the Alley Theatre while in high school in Houston, Texas, and later appeared in numerous prime-time shows, including *Hawaii Five-O* and *Gunsmoke*. On Broadway, she understudied in *Ladies at the Alamo* and received a Drama Desk nomination for her part in an off-Broadway revival of *Clash by Night*. She owns her own production company, Cheatham Continuation Corporation, as well as farms in Texas and in Vermont.

Michael Corbett
(Warren Carter)

This young Philadelphian studied international relations at the University of Pennsylvania before turning to acting, at which point he enrolled at the Boston Conservatory of Drama, Music and Dance. He appeared on Broadway in *Nefertiti*, and off-Broadway in *Matinee Kids* and *Bread and Circus* before joining the national touring company of *Grease*. He made his daytime debut on *Ryan's Hope* and joined *Search* in July 1982. Michael is six feet tall, was born under the sign of Gemini, and lives in Manhattan.

Larry Haines
(Stu Bergman)

Larry Haines joined the show shortly after its 1951 launch and over the past three decades has won two Emmy Awards, including one for outstanding daytime actor. He's also had a long radio career (some fifteen thousand performances) on shows such as *The Columbia Workshop*, *Inner Sanctum*, *Gangbusters*, and *Mike Hammer* (the latter in the title role). His prime-time appearances and stage work are also impressive and led to Tony Award nominations for *Promises* and *Generation*. Married to his high school sweetheart, Gertrude Halberstadt, he has one daughter, Debbie.

Sherry Mathis
(Liza Sentell)

Before making her daytime TV debut on *Search* in May 1978, the Memphis-born brunette appeared on Broadway in the Tony-winning musical, *A Little Night Music*. Later she played Olivia in another Broadway musical, *Music Is*. Indeed, she's appeared in some fifteen musicals as well as in several off-Broadway productions. A graduate of Memphis State University, Sherry studied in New York with Stella Adler and Carmine Gagliardi. She and her husband, actor Jerry Lanning, live in New York City.

Marcia McCabe
(Sunny Adamson)

Born in classy Bryn Mawr, outside Philadelphia, Marcia McCabe got into acting early (in fact, at age ten) and performed more than fifty roles in summer stock productions in Pennsylvania and in Maine. She studied theater at Rollins College in Florida and attended the American Academy of Dramatic Arts. She was a talk show host for a while on a local cable show, *Cue on View*, and made her daytime debut on *As the World Turns* before coming to *Search* in October 1978.

Lisa Peluso
(Wendy Wilkins McNeil)

Philadelphia-born Lisa Peluso will be twenty years old in July 1984. She joined the cast of *Search* when she was thirteen, but by then she was already an old-timer on TV, having acted since age four (a baby powder commercial). A graduate of the Professional Children's School in New York City, she appeared on Broadway in *Gypsy*, off-Broadway in *Sweet Sound of Trumpets*, and in the film *Saturday Night Fever* as John Travolta's younger sister, Linda. She's also a veteran of daytime dramas, having acted in *Somerset*, *As the World Turns*, and *Love of Life*. When is this girl going to get off her duff and *do* something?

Mary Stuart
(Joanne Tourneur)

The independent-minded Mary Stuart, now in her mid-fifties, was born, appropriately, on the Fourth of July, in Miami. After high school in Tulsa, Oklahoma, she worked as a camera girl at the venerable Hotel Roosevelt in New York City, where she was discovered by producer Joe Pasternak and signed to an MGM contract. She did a number of movies at MGM, including *The Hucksters* with Clark Gable and *The Adventures of Don Juan* with Errol Flynn, before deciding to audition for a role in an upcoming TV serial to be called *Search for Tomorrow*. She's been playing the leading role of Joanne Tourneur since the show's launch on September 3, 1951, and is the only member of that original cast still with the show.

Arrivals and Departures

Craig Augustine
(Keith McNeil)

The hazel-eyed, six-foot-three-inch actor was born in Wisconsin on October 31, 1957, and came to New York City in 1981 to take on the acting world. After an off-off-Broadway role in *In the Matter of J. Robert Oppenheimer*, Craig made his daytime TV debut on *Edge of Night*. Then in July 1982 he came to *Search*, leaving in the spring of 1983. Craig is single and lives in Manhattan.

Philip Brown
(Steve Kendall)

As a youngster, Phil Brown appeared for three seasons as Doris Day's son on her TV series. Later, the tall blue-eyed actor racked up a number of prime-time credits, including appearances on *The Love Boat* and *The Dukes of Hazzard*. One of the TV movies he appeared in is *Special Olympics*, and in fact Phil does volunteer work with the Special Olympics program. He made his daytime debut on *Days of Our Lives*, and he joined *Search* in May 1983. He's single and lives in New York City.

David Forsyth
(Hogan McLeary)

Tall, athletic, blue-eyed David Forsyth joined *Search* in the fall of 1983 after an impressively varied career in theater, commercials, industrial films, and television—the latter on ABC's *One Life to Live*. He was also on *Texas* for a year and a half. Born in Long Beach, California, David traveled extensively in Southeast Asia and Central America courtesy, as he puts it, of the U.S. Government. After leaving the Service, he played a number of stage roles, in such plays as *Sweet Charity*, *The Mousetrap* and *Any Wednesday*. Forsyth was trained as an underwater rescue specialist and loves "all marine activities," including sailing and air boating.

Cindy Gibb
(Suzi Wyatt Carter)

Twenty-year-old Cindy Gibb left *Search* in August 1983, after two years on the show. The Vermont-born actress graduated from high school in Westport, Connecticut, where she studied voice, worked as a model, and attended a theater workshop. She played an off-Broadway role in *Nathaniel* and made a brief appearance in the Woody Allen film, *Stardust Memories*. The five-foot-four-inch actress plays violin and piano, does jazz dancing, tap, and ballet, and models for the teen division of the Ford Model Agency.

Marcus Smythe
(Dane Taylor)

Marcus Smythe made his daytime debut in *Guiding Light* before coming to *Search* in June 1981, for a stint which came to an end in spring of 1983. The tall (six-foot-four-inch) actor went to college in his home state of Ohio before landing off-Broadway roles in *Tunnel Fever*, *Tenderloin*, and *Emigres*. He's played in the Los Angeles Globe Playhouse and the Champlain Shakespeare Festival, and has appeared in several TV series, including *Eight Is Enough* and *Operation Petticoat*. Marcus lives in New York City and likes jogging and skydiving.

Elizabeth Swackhamer
(Suzi Wyatt Carter)

On August 26, 1983, Elizabeth Swackhamer took over Cindy Gibb's part as Suzi Carter on *Search*, and she left the show by the end of the year. It was her first television role. Her background is primarily that of a dancer, with tap dancing as her specialty, but she acted in regional theater productions of *Getting Out*, *Barefoot in the Park*, and other plays. Born in Manhattan and raised in Connecticut, Elizabeth is the daughter of E.W. Swackhamer, a veteran Hollywood director.

Daytime Drama Emmy Awards

As usual, ABC came away with the bulk of the daytime Emmys, causing much grumbling at the other two networks about ABC's tactics. CBS and NBC spokesmen complain that ABC buys memberships for many of its daytime people in the National Academy of Television Arts and Sciences (NATAS) and that these folks vote in a bloc for ABC shows. An ABC spokesperson calls that "a ludicrous statement." ABC people are "encouraged" to join, says the spokesman, but each person must pay for his or her own membership. And they're free to vote for whomever they want.

Here's the way the voting went in 1983:

Outstanding Daytime Drama
The Young and the Restless (CBS)

Outstanding Actor
Robert S. Woods (Bo Buchanan on ABC's *One Life to Live*)

Outstanding Actress
Dorothy Lyman (Opal Garner on ABC's *All My Children*)

Outstanding Actor in a Supporting Role
Darnell Williams (Jesse Hubbard on ABC's *All My Children*)

Oustanding Actress in a Supporting Role
Louise Shaffer (Rae Woodard on ABC's *Ryan's Hope*)

Outstanding Direction for a Daytime Drama Series
Allen Fristoe, Norman Hall, Peter Miner, David Pressman from ABC's *One Life to Live*

Outstanding Writing
Claire Labine, Paul Avila Mayer, Mary Ryan Munisteri, Eugene Price, Judith Pinsker, Nancy Ford, B. K. Perlman, Rory Metcalf, Trent Jones from ABC's *Ryan's Hope*

Outstanding Achievement in Technical Excellence (an Entire Series)
ABC's **All My Children**

Outstanding Achievement in Technical Excellence (a Particular Episode)
The episode of CBS's **Guiding Light** shot in New Hampshire

Outstanding Achievement in Design
ABC's **All My Children**

Cast of Characters

Mariann Aalda
Didi Bannister, Edge of Night

Willie Aames
Robbie Hamlin, Edge of Night

Jay Acavone
Brian Emerson, Search for Tomorrow

Deborah Adair
Jill Foster Abbott, The Young and the Restless

Julie Adams
Paula Denning, Capitol

Marla Adams
Dina Abbott Mergeron, The Young and the Restless

Wesley Addy
Cabot Alden, Loving

Rose Alaio
Helen Manzini, Guiding Light

Grant Aleksander
Philip Spaulding, Guiding Light

Denise Alexander
Dr. Lesley Webber, General Hospital

Kristian Alfonso
Hope Williams, Days of Our Lives

Jed Allan
Don Craig, Days of Our Lives

Elizabeth Allen
Dr. Gwen Harding, Guiding Light

Nancy Addison Altman
Jillian Coleridge, Ryan's Hope

Rachel Ames
Audrey Hobart, General Hospital

William Andrews
George Fenton, Another World

John Aniston
Martin Tourneur, Search for Tomorrow

Gerald Anthony
Marco Dane, One Life to Live

Lewis Arlt
David Thatcher, Another World

Mark Arnold
Gavin Wylie, Edge of Night

Rod Arrants
Travis Tourneur Sentell, Search for Tomorrow

Jennifer Ashe
Lily Slater, Loving

Craig Augustine
Keith McNeil, Search for Tomorrow

Phylicia Ayers-Allen
Courtney Wright, One Life to Live

Leah Ayres
Valerie Bryson, Edge of Night

B

Hillary Bailey
Margo Montgomery Hughes, As the World Turns

Christine Baranski
Beverly Tucker, Another World

Andrea Barber
Carrie Brady, Days of Our Lives

Evalyn Baron
Miss Devon, Another World

Julia Barr
Brooke Cudahy, All My Children

Bernard Barrow
Johnny Ryan, Ryan's Hope

Charita Bauer
Bert Bauer, Guiding Light

Amanda Bearse
Amanda, All My Children

Kimberly Beck-Hilton
Julie Clegg, Capitol

Kabir Bedi
Lord Rama, General Hospital

Gregory Beecroft
Tony Reardon, Guiding Light

Sam Behrens
Jake Meyer, General Hospital

Richard Bekins
Jamie Frame, Another World

Meg Bennett
Julia Newman, The Young and the Restless

Dawn Benz
Sally Frame, Another World

John Beradino
Dr. Steven Hardy, General Hospital

Richard Bergman
Brett Fredericks, Days of Our Lives

Peter Bergman
Dr. Cliff Warner, All My Children

Christopher Bernau
Alan Spaulding, Guiding Light

Jack Betts
Louis St. George, Another World

Bill Beyers
Wally McCandless, Capitol

Susan Bigelow
Barbara, Edge of Night

Dick Billingsley
Scotty Banning, Days of Our Lives

Loanne Bishop
Rose Kelly, General Hospital

Pamela Blair
Rita Mae Bristow, Loving

Mary Lynn Blanks
Annie Ward, As the World Turns

Judith Blazer
Ariel Dixon, As the World Turns

Brian Bloom
Dustin Donovan, As the World Turns

Vasili Bogazianos
Benny Sago, All My Children

Steve Bond
Jimmy Lee Holt, General Hospital

Richard Borg
Spencer Varney, Edge of Night

Eric Braeden
Victor Newman, The Young and the Restless

Victor Brandt
Danny Donato, Capitol

Tracey Bregman
Lauren Fenmore, The Young and the Restless

Dick Briggs
Thomas Mendenhall, Ryan's Hope

Philip Brown
Steve McNeil, Search for Tomorrow

Roger Aaron Brown
Danny Grant, Days of Our Lives

Peter Brown
Roger Forbes, General Hospital

Gail Brown
Clarice Ewing, Another World

Lisa Brown
Nola Chamberlain, Guiding Light

Susan Brown
Dr. Gail Adamson, General Hospital

Patricia Bruder
Ellen Stewart, As the World Turns

Catherine Bruno
Nora Fulton, Edge of Night

Ed Bryce
Bill Bauer, Guiding Light

Scott Bryce
Craig Montgomery, As the World Turns

Larry Bryggman
Dr. John Dixon, As the World Turns

Shelly Burch
Delila Buchanan, One Life to Live

Danielle Burns
Nancy McGowan, Another World

Warren Burton
Warren Andrews, Guiding Light

Ruth Buzzi
Leticia, Days of Our Lives

Reggie Rock Bythewood
R. J. Morgan, Another World

Rory Calhoun
Judson Tyler, Capitol

Anthony Call
Herb Callison, One Life to Live

Kay Campbell
Kate Martin, All My Children

Alan Campbell
Evan Grant, Another World

David Canary
Steven Frame, Another World

Macdonald Carey
Tom Horton, Days of Our Lives

Philip Carey
Asa Buchanan, One Life to Live

Ronn Carroll
Stan Hathaway, Edge of Night

Michael Catlin
Dr. Thomas McCandless, Capitol

Lane Caudell
Woody King, Days of Our Lives

Lee Chamberlain
Pat Baxter, All My Children

Jeff Chamberlain
Lawrence Barrington, Capitol

Judith Chapman
Charlotte Greer Ryan, Ryan's Hope

Leslie Charleson
Dr. Monica Quartermaine, General Hospital

Marie Cheatham
Stephanie Wyatt, Search for Tomorrow

Marilyn Chris
Wanda Wolek, One Life to Live

Templeton Christopher
Carol Robbins, The Young and the Restless

Richard Clark
Bryan Lister, Guiding Light

Carolyn Ann Clark
Lesley Ann Monroe, Guiding Light

Josh Clark
Bert Keller, Another World

Marsha Clark
Hillary Bauer, Guiding Light

John Clarke
Mickey Horton, Days of Our Lives

Patrick James Clarke
Dr. Patrick Ryan, Ryan's Hope

Jordan Clarke
Billy Lewis, Guiding Light

Brian Patrick Clarke
Dr. Grant Putnam, General Hospital

Robert Clary
Robert LeClair, Days of Our Lives

Alan Coates
Ian Devereaux, Edge of Night

Drew Coburn
Barry Durrell, Another World

Robert Colbert
Stuart Brooks, The Young and the Restless

Margaret Colin
Margo Montgomery Hughes, As the World Turns

Booth Colman
Dr. Hector Jerrold, General Hospital

David Combs
Sgt. Bill Gorman, Another World

Forrest Compton
Mike Carr, Edge of Night

Norma Connolly
Ruby Anderson, General Hospital

Carolyn Conwell
Mary Williams, The Young and the Restless

Jennifer Cooke
Morgan Nelson, Guiding Light

Roderick Cooke
Tango, One Life to Live

Jeanne Cooper
Katherine Chancellor, The Young and the Restless

Michael Corbett
Warren Carter, Search for Tomorrow

Melinda Cordell
Natalie Dearborn, General Hospital

Nicholas Coster
Anthony Makana, One Life to Live

Geraldine Court
Jennifer Evans, Guiding Light

Jacquie Courtney
Pat Ashley, One Life to Live

Matthew Cowles
Lonnie, As the World Turns

Cusie Cram
Cassie Callison, One Life to Live

Barbara Crampton
Trista Evans, Days of Our Lives

Bryan Cranston
Douglas Donovan, Loving

Joel Crothers
Dr. Miles Cavanaugh, Edge of Night

Kathleen Cullen
Amanda Spaulding, Guiding Light

Steven Culp
Dan Wolek, One Life to Live

Chris Cunningham
Kevin Riley, One Life to Live

John Cunningham
Garth Slater, Loving

Todd Curtis
Jordy Clegg, Capitol

D

Augusta Dabney
Isabelle Alden, Loving

Arlene Dahl
Lucinda Schneck, One Life to Live

Irene Dailey
Liz Matthews, Another World

Susanna Dalton
Dr. Sally Perkins, All My Children

Michael Damian
Danny Romalotti, The Young and the Restless

Stuart Damon
Dr. Alan Quartermaine, General Hospital

David Mason Daniels
Tyler McCandless, Capitol

Linda Dano
Felicia Gallant, Another World

Randy Danson
Miss Rose, Another World

Marty Davich
Marty the pianist, Days of Our Lives

Doug Davidson
Paul Williams, The Young and the Restless

Eileen Davidson
Ashley Abbott, The Young and the Restless

Brian Davies
Scott, One Life to Live

Peter Davies
Father Jim Vochek, Loving

Todd Davis
Bryan Phillips, General Hospital

Jerry Davis
Tracey Winthrop, Another World

Ricky Dawson
Lee Stewart, As the World Turns

Justin Deas
Tom Hughes, As the World Turns

Gloria DeHaven
Bess Shelby, Ryan's Hope

John deLancie
Eugene Bradford, Days of Our Lives

Kim Delaney
Jenny Gardner, All My Children

Robert Desiderio
Steven Piermont, One Life to Live

Cain DeVore
Danny Walton, Search for Tomorrow

Kristine de Bell
Pam Warren, The Young and the Restless

Shirley de Burgh
Delia Abernathy, Days of Our Lives

Brenda Dickson
Jill Foster Abbott, The Young and the Restless

Ellen Dolan
Maureen Bauer, Guiding Light

Alex Donnelly
Diane Jenkins, The Young and the Restless

Jerry Douglas
John Abbott, The Young and the Restless

Ronald Drake
Jasper Sloane, All My Children

Olympia Dukakis
Barbara Moreno, Search for Tomorrow

Christopher Durham
Matt McCandless, Capitol

Marj Dusay
Myrna Clegg, Capitol

Jenny Rebecca Dweir
Ryan Fenelli, Ryan's Hope

E

Candice Earley
Donna Cortlandt, All My Children

Christine Ebersole
Maxie McDermot, One Life to Live

Louis Edmonds
Langley Wallingford, All My Children

Richard Egan
Sam Clegg II, Capitol

Shannon Eubanks
Ann Alden Forbes, Loving

Judi Evans
Beth Raiens, Guiding Light

Michael Evans
Douglas Austin, The Young and the Restless

Dillon Evans
Reginald Fearing, Another World

Andrea Evans-Massey
Patty Williams Abbott, The Young and the Restless

Geoffrey Ewing
Dist. Atty. Adam Banks, Another World

F

Jeff Fahey
Gary Corelli, One Life to Live

Sandy Faison
Dr. Beth Corell, Edge of Night

Antonio Fargas
Les Baxter, All My Children

Jose Ferrer
Reuben Marino, Another World

Mary Fickett
Ruth Martin, All My Children

Larry Fleischman
Ringo Altman, Search for Tomorrow

Steven Fletcher
Brad Vernon, One Life to Live

Charles Flohe
"Preacher" Emerson, Edge of Night

Ann Flood
Nancy Karr, Edge of Night

Steven Ford
Andy Richards, The Young and the Restless

Faith Ford
Julia Shearer, Another World

Constance Ford
Ada Hobson, Another World

Tisha M. Ford
Mary Sue Morgan, Another World

David Forsyth
Hogan McLeary, Search for Tomorrow
Burke Donovan, As the World Turns

Henderson Forsythe
Dr. David Stewart, As the World Turns

Don Frabotta
Dave the waiter, Days of Our Lives

Genie Francis
Laura Baldwin Spencer, General Hospital

Nancy Frangione
Cecile dePoulignac, Another World

Hugh Franklin
Dr. Charles Tyler, All My Children

Elizabeth Franz
Alma Rudder, Another World

Mark Frazer
Prince, Another World

Morgan Freeman
Roy Bingham, Another World

Al Freeman, Jr.
Capt. Ed Hall, One Life to Live

Josh Freund
Josh Moreno, Search for Tomorrow

David Froman
Gunther Wagner, Edge of Night

Eileen Fulton
Lisa McColl, As the World Turns

Sharon Gabet
Raven Whitney, Edge of Night

John Gabriel
Dr. Seneca Beaulac, Ryan's Hope

Sandy Gabriel
Edna Thornton, All My Children

David Gale
Rusty Sentell, Search for Tomorrow

Helen Gallagher
Maeve Ryan, Ryan's Hope

Joe Gallison
Dr. Neil Curtis, Days of Our Lives

June Daly Gamble
Kelly Harper, Capitol

Duncan Gamble
Frank Burgess, Capitol

Beulah Garrick
Violet Renfield, Guiding Light

Larry Gates
H. B. Lewis, Guiding Light

Jennifer Gatti
Angela Moreno, Search for Tomorrow

Anthony Geary
Luke Spencer, General Hospital

Robert Gentry
Giles, One Life to Live

Anthony George
Will Vernon, One Life to Live

Robert Gerringer
Del Emerson, Edge of Night

Cynthia Gibb
Suzi Wyatt Carter, Search for Tomorrow

Linda Gibboney
Jenny Deacon, Search for Tomorrow

Stacey Glick
Andy McNeil, Search for Tomorrow

John Glover
Vargas, Search for Tomorrow

Lee Godart
Kent Bogard, All My Children

Deborah Goodrich
Silver Kane (Connie Wilkes), All My Children

Gerold Gordon
Dr. Mark Dante, General Hospital

Gordon Gould
Haywood, Another World

Sally Gracie
Ina Hopkins, One Life to Live

Leslie Graves
Brenda Clegg, Capitol

Velekka Gray
Dr. Sharon Reaves/Ruby Collins, The Young and the Restless

Kim Morgan Greene
Nicole Love, Another World

Robin Greer
Sidney Rice, Ryan's Hope

Janet Grey
Eve McFarren, Guiding Light

Carmine Grey
Cory Ewing, Another World

Donald Groh
Donald Lewis Brock, General Hospital

Malcolm Groome
Dr. Patrick Ryan, Ryan's Hope

Ava Haddad
Cassie Callison, One Life to Live

Brett Hadley
Carl Williams, The Young and the Restless

Larry Haines
Stu Bergman, Search for Tomorrow

Ron Hale
Dr. Roger Coleridge, Ryan's Hope

Grayson Hall
Euphemia, One Life to Live

Deidre Hall
Dr. Marlena Evans-Brady, Days of Our Lives

Ben Hammer
Alex Morgan, The Young and the Restless

Peter Hansen
Lee Baldwin, General Hospital

Harriet Harris
Cathy Harris, Another World

Jackee Harry
Lily Mason, Another World

Tim Hart
Simon, One Life to Live

Peter Haskell
Lloyd Kendall, Search for Tomorrow
Hollis Kirkland, Ryan's Hope

Don Hastings
Dr. Bob Hughes, As the World Turns

Bob Hastings
Capt. Ramsey, General Hospital

Eddie Earl Hatch
Tucker Foster, As the World Turns

Susan Seaforth Hayes
Julie Williams, Days of Our Lives

Bill Hayes
Doug Williams, Days of Our Lives

Lillian Hayman
Sadie Gray, One Life to Live

Kathryn Hays
Kim Andropolous, As the World Turns

Frances Heflin
Mona Tyler, All My Children

Marg Helgenberger
Siobhan Novak, Ryan's Hope

Benjamin Hendrickson
Sgt. Bartlett, Another World

Michael Hennessy
Joe Novak, Ryan's Hope

Eileen Herlie
Myrtle Fargate, All My Children

Anthony Herrera
James Stenbeck, As the World Turns
Dane Hammond, Loving

Catherine Hickland
Julie Clegg McCandless, Capitol

Lise Hilboldt
Janet Singleton, Another World

Roger Hill
Alec Lowndes, One Life to Live

Earl Hindman
Bob Ried, Ryan's Hope

Patricia Hodges
Maisie, Another World

Christoper Holder
Kevin Bancroft, The Young and the Restless

Randy Holland
Rick Daros, The Young and the Restless

Rebecca Hollen
Trish Lewis, Guiding Light

Ellen Holly
Carla Scott, One Life to Live

Avra Holt
Bobbi Maxwell, As the World Turns

Robert Horton
Whit McColl, As the World Turns

Leann Hunley
Anna Brady-DiMera, Days of Our Lives

John Hutton
Peter Love, Another World

I

Lela Ivey
Mitzi Martin, Edge of Night

J

Christopher Jarrett
Damien Tyler, Edge of Night

Tina Johnson
Rhonda Sue Huckaby, Search for Tomorrow

Christine Jones
Catsy Krikland, Ryan's Hope

Linda C. Jones
Rita Kent, Another World

Carolyn Jones
Myrna Clegg, Capitol

Stephen Joyce
Eli Sims, Guiding Light

K

Patricia Kalember
Merrill Vochek, Loving

Teri Keane
Rose Donovan, Loving

Noah Keen
Patrick Donovan, Loving

Susan Keith
Shana, Loving

Mary Keller
Amanda Kirkland, Ryan's Hope

Mary Page Keller
Sally Frame, Another World

Shell Kepler
Amy Vining, General Hospital

Jay Kerr
Brian Forbes, The Young and the Restless

Anne Kerry
Janet Singleton, Another World

Lois Kibbee
Geraldine Saxon, Edge of Night

James Kiberd
Mike Donovan, Loving

Jason Kincaid
Sam Brady, All My Children

Kathleen King
Gretchen, Days of Our Lives

Maeve Kinkead
Vanessa Chamberlain, Guiding Light

Dana Klaboe
Amanda Cory, Another World

Margaret Klenck
Edwina Lewis, One Life to Live

Michael Knight
Tad Gardner, All My Children

Harley Kozak
Annabelle Sims, Guiding Light

Philip Kraus
Mr. Barrows, Another World

Ilene Kristen
Delia Coleridge, Ryan's Hope

L

Felicity LaFortune
Leigh Kirkland, Ryan's Hope

Caroline Lagerfelt
Patricia, Edge of Night

Michael LaGuardia
Cullen, Another World

Joe Lambie
Gregory Malko, General Hospital

CAST OF CHARACTERS

Mark LaMura
Mark Dalton, All My Children

Sophia Landon
Jennifer Thatcher, Another World

Laurence Lau
Greg Nelson, All My Children

Elizabeth Lawrence
Myra Murdoch , All My Children

Lee Lawson
Bea Reardon, Guiding Light

Mary Layne
Camilla Devereaux, Edge of Night

Chris LeBlanc
Kirk McColl, As the World Turns

Jonna Lee
Julia Shearer, Another World

Irving Lee
Calvin Stoner, Edge of Night

Anna Lee
Lila Quartermaine, General Hospital

Roberta Leighton
Shirley Pickett, General Hospital

Michael Leon
Pete Jennings, Days of Our Lives

Terry Lester
Jack Abbott, The Young and the Restless

Suzanne Leuffen
Shelley Johnson, One Life to Live

Michael Levin
Jack Fenelli, Ryan's Hope

David Lewis
Edward Quartermaine, General Hospital

Judith Light
Karen Wolek, One Life to Live

Tom Ligon
Billy Bristow, Loving

Robert Lipton
Dr. Jeff Ward, As the World Turns

Mitch Litrofsky
Tom Bergman, Search for Tomorrow

Bradley Lockerman
Zed Diamond, Capitol

Dorian Lopinto
Samantha Vernon, One Life to Live

Gloria Loring
Liz Chandler, Days of Our Lives

Lisa Loring
Cricket Montgomery, As the World Turns

Lori Loughlin
Jody Travis, Edge of Night

Susan Lucci
Erica Kane, All My Children

Melissa Luciano
Jeanne Ewing, Another World

Robert LuPone
Tom Bergman, Search for Tomorrow

Dorothy Lyman
Opal Gardner, All My Children

Debbie Lytton
Melissa Anderson, Days of Our Lives

Ray MacDonnell
Dr. Joe Martin, All My Children

Billy Mack
Carl Blair, Jr., All My Children

Juanita Mahone
Samantha Jones, As the World Turns

Beth Maitland
Traci Abbott, The Young and the Restless

Larkin Malloy
Sky Whitney, Edge of Night

Laura Malone
Blaine Cory, Another World

Christopher Marcantel
Curtis Alden, Loving

Kelly Maroney
Kimberly Harris Beaulac, Ryan's Hope

Anne-Marie Martin
Gwen Davies, Days of Our Lives

W. T. Martin
Stan Holden, As the World Turns

John Martinuzzi
Stavros Cassadine, General Hospital

Gregg Marx
David Banning, Days of Our Lives

Joseph Mascolo
Stefano DiMera, Days of Our Lives

Margaret Mason
Eve, The Young and the Restless

Carmen Mathews
Bess Killworth, Another World

Sherry Mathis
Liza Sentell, Search for Tomorrow

Brian Matthews
Eric Garrison, The Young and the Restless

Robin Mattson
Heather Webber, General Hospital

Frank Maxwell
Dan Rooney, General Hospital

Marcia McCabe
Sunny Adamson, Search for Tomorrow

Julianna McCarthy
Elizabeth Foster Brooks, The Young and the Restless

Judith McConnell
Eva Vasquez, One Life to Live

Malachy McCourt
Levin MacGuiness, The Young and the Restless

Maeve McGuire
Elena dePoulignac, Another World

Marilyn McIntyre
Noreen Vochek Donovan, Loving

James McKrell
Dr. Parker, Capitol

Regan McManus
Mary Vernon Karr, One Life to Live

Matthew McNamara
Bobby, All My Children

Steve McNaughton
Gil, All My Children

Kathy McNeil
Karen Haines Stenbeck, As the World Turns

Kristen Meadows
Mimi, One Life to Live

Ken Meeker
Rafe Garretson, One Life to Live

Lee Meredith
Charmane L'Amour, As the World Turns

Jeanna Michaels
Constance Townley, General Hospital

Taylor Miller
Nina Warner, All My Children

Betty Miller
Jeanne Ewing, Another World

Robert Milli
Lars Bogard, All My Children

Michael Minor
Dr. Royal Dunning, Another World

James Mitchell
Palmer Cortlandt, All My Children

Susan Monts
Prof. Aja Doyan, Search for Tomorrow

William Mooney
Paul Martin, One Life to Live

Demi More
Jacki Templeton, General Hospital

Debbi Morgan
Angie Hubbard, All My Children

Karen Morris-Gowdy
Dr. Faith Coleridge, Ryan's Hope

Joe Morton
Dr. Abel Marsh/Leo Marsh, Another World

Deborah Mullowney
Sloane Denning, Capitol

Ariane Munker
Amanda Kirkland, Ryan's Hope

Peg Murray
Jeanne Ewing, Another World
Olga, All My Children

Mary Gordon Murray
Becky Buchanan, One Life to Live

Wolf Muser
Kurt Voightlander, Capitol

N

Hugo Napier
Gunnar Stenbeck, As the World Turns

Karen Needle
Poppy Johnson, Edge of Night

CAST OF CHARACTERS

Ed Nelson
Sen. Mark Denning, Capitol

Peter Nevins
David Snell, Edge of Night

Robert Newman
Josh Lewis, Guiding Light

Tom Nielson
Floyd Parker, Guiding Light

Kathleen Noone
Ellen Dalton, All My Children

Wayne Northrop
Roman Brady, Days of Our Lives

Gretchen Oehler
Vivien Gorrow, Another World

David Oliver
Perry Hutchins, Another World

Leslie O'Hara
Rebecca Cartwright, Guiding Light

Michael O'Leary
Rick Bauer, Guiding Light

Thomas O'Rourke
Dr. Justin Marler, Guiding Light

Petronia Paley
Quinn Harding, Another World

Scott Palmer
Prof. Tim Sullivan, The Young and the Restless

Dennis Parker
Derek Mallory, Edge of Night

Norman Parker
David Cameron, Edge of Night

Dawn Parrish
Ronnie Angelo, Capitol

Julie Parrish
Maggie Brady, Capitol

Will Patton
Ox Knowles, Ryan's Hope

Lisa Peluso
Wendy Wilkins McNeil, Search for Tomorrow

Denise Pence
Katie Parker, Guiding Light

Thaao Penghlis
Antony DiMera, Days of Our Lives

Alexander Perker
Matthew Cory, Another World

Jacques Perreault
Frank Andropolous, As the World Turns

Brock Peters
Frank Lewis, The Young and the Restless

Lenka Peterson
Marie Fenton, Another World

Geoffrey Pierson
Frank Ryan, Ryan's Hope

Gene Pietragallo
Brian Emerson, Search for Tomorrow

Danny Pintauro
Paul Stenbeck, As the World Turns

Mark Pinter
Mark Evans, Guiding Light

Roy Poole
Neil MacCurtain, Ryan's Hope

Richard J. Porter
Larry Ewing, Another World

Susan Pratt
Dr. Claire Ramsey, Guiding Light

Elaine Princi
Miranda Hughes, As the World Turns

Tricia Pursley
Devan McFadden, All My Children

Sheryl Lee Ralph
Mac, Search for Tomorrow

Dack Rambo
Steve Jacobi, All My Children

Mary Linda Rapelye
Maggie Crawford, As the World Turns

Marguerite Ray
Mamie, The Young and the Restless

James Rebhorn
Bradley Raines, Guiding Light

Peter Reckell
Bo Brady, Days of Our Lives

Quinn Redeker
Alex Marshall, Days of Our Lives

Joyce Reehling
Linda Taggert, Another World

Frances Reid
Alice Horton, Days of Our Lives

Luke Reilly
Ted Bancroft, Another World

James Reynolds
Abe Carver, Days of Our Lives

Madlyn Rhue
Daphne DiMera, Days of Our Lives

Christopher Rich
Sandy Cory, Another World

Trevor Richards
Kevin Thatcher, Another World

Clint Ritchie
Clint Buchanan, One Life to Live

Kaitlin Roark
Maggie Cory, Another World

DeAnna Robbins
Cindy Lake, The Young and the Restless

Chris Robinson
Dr. Rick Webber, General Hospital

William Roerick
Henry Chamberlain, Guiding Light

Suzanne Rogers
Maggie Horton, Days of Our Lives

Tristan Rogers
Robert Scorpio, General Hospital

Kimberly Ross
Amy Burke, Capitol

Natalie Ross
Enid Nelson, All My Children

Merri Lynn Ross
Emma Lutz, General Hospital

Elvera Roussel
Hope Spaulding, Guiding Light

Pamela Roylance
Sandy Horton, Days of Our Lives

Frank Runyeon
Steve Andropolous, As the World Turns

Jennifer Runyon
Sally Frame, Another World

Leon Russom
Dr. Zachary Stone, As the World Turns

Meg Ryan
Betsy Stewart Montgomery, As the World Turns

S

Emma Samms
Holly Sutton, General Hospital

Philece Sampler
Renee Banning, Days of Our Lives

Rodney Saulsberry
Jeff Johnson, Capitol

Lanna Saunders
Marie Curtis, Days of Our Lives

Michael Scalera
Joey Martin, All My Children

Susan Scannell
Kristen Carter Emerson, Search for Tomorrow

Damion Scheller
Josh Moreno, Search for Tomorrow

Stephen Schnetzer
Cass Winthrop, Another World

Nicole Schrank
Maggie Cory, Another World

Jean Bruce Scott
Jessica Horton, Days of Our Lives

David Sederholm
Bill Hyde, Ryan's Hope

Kyra Sedgwick
Julia Shearer, Another World

John Seitz
Zack Hill, Another World

Louise Shaffer
Rae Woodard, Ryan's Hope

Michele Shay
Henrietta Morgan, Another World

John Shearin
Roger Forbes, Loving

CAST OF CHARACTERS

John Wesley Shipp
Dr. Kelly Nelson, Guiding Light

Richard Shoberg
Tom Cudahy, All My Children

Pamela Shoemaker
Shelley Franklyn, Edge of Night

Kin Shriner
Scotty Baldwin, General Hospital

Peter Simon
Dr. Ed Bauer, Guiding Light

Craig Sisler
Alan Lewis, Another World

Jeremy Slate
Chuck Wilson, One Life to Live

Erika Slezak
Victoria Buchanan, One Life to Live

Lisa Sloan
Nicole Cavanaugh, Edge of Night

Tina Sloan
Lillian Raines, Guiding Light

James Sloyan
Mitch Bronsky, Ryan's Hope

Thomas Sminkey
Harold Loomis, All My Children

Lois Smith
Ella Fitz, Another World

Marcus Smythe
Dane Taylor, Search for Tomorrow

Norman Snow
Richard Fairchild III, As the World Turns

Nancy Snyder
Katrina Karr, One Life to Live

Sheila Spencer
Thomasina Harding, Another World

Gillian Spencer
Daisy Cortlandt, All My Children

Rick Springfield
Noah Drake, General Hospital

John Stamos
Blackie Parrish, General Hospital

Michael Stark
Sully, Edge of Night

Todd Starks
Roge Avery, Capitol

Jadrien Steel
Little John Ryan, Ryan's Hope

Perry Stephens
Jack Forbes, Loving

Lilibet Stern
Patty Williams Abbott, The Young and the Restless

Shawn Stevens
Oliver Martin, Days of Our Lives

Paul Stevens
Brian Bancroft, Another World

Doug Stevenson
Lee Sentell, Search for Tomorrow

Catherine Mary Stewart
Kayla Brady, Days of Our Lives

Don Stewart
Michael Bauer, Guiding Light

Michael Storm
Larry Wolek, One Life to Live

Carl Strano
Max, The Young and the Restless

Robin Strasser
Dorian Callison, One Life to Live

Mary Stuart
Joanne Tourneur, Search for Tomorrow

Anna Stuart
Donna Love, Another World

Jon St. Elwood
Jazz, The Young and the Restless

Tom Sullivan
Michael Kendall, Search for Tomorrow

Nicholas Surovy
Michael Roy, All My Children

Elizabeth Swackhamer
Suzi Wyatt Carter, Search for Tomorrow

Anne Sward
Lyla Montgomery, As the World Turns

T

Mark Tapscott
Earl Bancroft, The Young and the Restless

Josh Taylor
Chris Kositchek, Days of Our Lives

248

Lauren-Marie Taylor
Stacey Donovan, Loving

Jennifer Taylor
Chris Egan, Edge of Night

Joseph Taylor
Tony DiSalvo, The Young and the Restless

Frank Telfer
Brian McColl, As the World Turns

Krista Tesreau
Mindy Lewis, Guiding Light

Kristine Thatcher
Miss Steiner, Another World

Brynn Thayer
Jenny Janssen, One Life to Live

Lynne Thigpen
Aunt Flora Baxter, All My Children

Robin Thomas
Mark Singleton, Another World

Melody Thomas
Nikki Reed Bancroft, The Young and the Restless

Cali Timmons
Maggie Shelby, Ryan's Hope

Bill Timoney
Alfred Vanderpoole, All My Children

Wayne Tippit
Ted Adamson, Search for Tomorrow

Marissa Tomei
Marcy Thompson, As the World Turns

Thomas Toner
Horace Bakewell, Another World

Constance Towers
Clarissa McCandless, Capitol

Ernie Townsend
Cliff Nelson, Edge of Night

Lisa Trusel
Melissa Anderson, Days of Our Lives

Michael Tylo
Quinton Chamberlain, Guiding Light

U

Kim Ulrich
Diana McColl, As the World Turns

V

Tasia Valenza
Dottie Thornton, All My Children

Terri Vandenbosch
Frannie Hughes, As the World Turns

Richard Van Vleet
Dr. Chuck Tyler, All My Children

Jerry ver Dorn
Ross Marler, Guiding Light

John Vickery
Richard Scanlon, Edge of Night

Betsy von Furstenberg
Lisa McColl, As the World Turns

Danielle von Zerneck
Louisa (Lou) Swenson, General Hospital

W

Tim Waldrip
Danny Wolek, One Life to Live

Tonja Walker
Lisbeth Bachman, Capitol

Nichols Walker
Sam "Trey" Clegg III, Capitol

Marcy Walker
Liza Colby, All My Children

Susan Walters
Lorna Forbes, Loving

Ruth Warrick
Phoebe Wallingford, All My Children

Douglass Watson
Mackenzie Cory, Another World

Chris Weatherhead
Alicia Van Dine, Edge of Night

Patty Weaver
Gina Roma, The Young and the Restless

A. C. Wery
Dick Grant, One Life to Live

Kathleen Widdoes
Una MacCurtain, Ryan's Hope

CAST OF CHARACTERS

Tom Wiggin
Gil Fenton, Another World

Donna Wilkes
Pamela, Days of Our Lives

Lisa Wilkinson
Nancy Grant, All My Children

Kate Wilkinson
Mrs. Franklin, Another World

Ann Williams
Ann Slater, Loving

Darnell Williams
Jesse Hubbard, All My Children

Stephanie E. Williams
Amy Lewis, The Young and the Restless

Sherilyn Wolter
Celia Quartermaine, General Hospital

Lana Wood
Fran Burke, Capitol

Lynn Wood
Alison Bancroft, The Young and the Restless

Robert S. Woods
Bo Buchanan, One Life to Live

Michael Woods
Dr. John Stevens, Guiding Light

Tom Wright
John Carver Colton, Jr., Search for Tomorrow

Sharon Wyatt
Tiffany Hill, General Hospital

Victoria Wyndham
Rachel Cory, Another World

Y

Stephen Yates
Jamie Frame, Another World

Z

Jerry Zaks
Louis Van Dine, Edge of Night

Michael Zaslow
David Renaldi (Reynolds), One Life to Live

Jacklyn Zeman
Bobbie Spencer, R.N., General Hospital

Colleen Zenk
Barbara Stenbeck, As the World Turns

Kim Zimmer
Echo Di Savoy, One Life to Live
Riva Lewis, Guiding Light